Enjoy Investing on the Stock Exchange

To Robyn

Enjoy Investing on the Stock Exchange

KARL POSEL Ph.D. D.Sc. (Eng.)
Mathematical Investment Consultant
Formerly Professor of Applied Mathematics
University of Durban-Westville

BUTTERWORTHS
DURBAN

Butterworths
Professional Publishers (Pty) Ltd
Reg No 87/03997/07

ISBN 0 409 10262 8

Durban
8 Walter Place, Waterval Park
Mayville 4091

Johannesburg
108 Elizabeth Avenue
Benmore 2010

Pretoria
301 Telkor Building
270 Main Street
Waterkloof 0181

Cape Town
3 Gardens Business Village, Hope Street
Cape Town 8001

Typeset by Positone Pinetown
Printed and bound by Interpak (Natal) Pietermaritzburg
The imprint Butterworths is used under licence

Foreword

In *Enjoy Investing on the Stock Exchange*, Dr Karl Posel, a former professor of applied mathematics, sets out to show that correct Stock Exchange investment is not gambling and that an investor can (and should) actually enjoy his operations on the Stock Exchange.

After very detailed repetition of his nine laws to be strictly adhered to by ardent investors, first propounded in *Winning on the JSE*, Dr Posel concentrates on the tax implications of the investor's activities on the Stock Exchange. As he shows, this topic is sufficiently complex to have been omitted from his earlier work. He defines 'capital assets' and 'revenue assets' and refers the reader to judgments in tax cases to indicate which of his share transactions may be of a capital nature and which of a revenue nature, and hence will or will not attract tax on the realised profits.

Dr Posel's treatment of the complex subject of the sale of shares in order to retain their required capital asset definition is the most detailed I have come across in my reading on the subject, and the reader will find the references given to tax cases most interesting and enlightening.

B SHAPIRO
Member of the Johannesburg Stock Exchange

Contents

PART 1

Cultivating the desirable character trait of confidence

1

Correct Stock Exchange investment is highly erudite

Page

1.1 Introduction

My late father was a cost accountant. Up until the day he died, in 1982 at the age of 85, he refused to place ten cents on the Stock Exchange. Throughout my childhood he drummed it into me that there were three ways to lose money: on women, on horses and on the Stock Exchange. Women were the nicest, horses the fastest and the Stock Exchange the surest!

In those days there was greyhound racing at the old Wanderers ground in Johannesburg on Friday nights, and gamblers went to the horse racing at Turffontein on Wednesdays and Saturdays, to the greyhound racing at the Wanderers on Fridays, and to the Johannesburg Stock Exchange on the days in between! Purchases of shares were based on 'tips' from those in the know. The barber's chair featured prominently in the origination and dissemination of such tips. Often a haircut was accompanied by apparently sage advice, whispered in a suitably impressive tone of voice by the wielder of the scissors: 'Merriespruit is a certainty. I have it on good authority that it cannot fail.' To anyone growing up in this climate, the words 'Stock Exchange' were synonymous with 'Gambling Den'. Unfortunately, it would appear that many of the 1989 generation still hold this point of view.

I do not know whether my intense interest in the Stock Exchange as a *mathematical* sphere of investment arose in rebellion against my father. Whatever the case, this interest commenced with the 1968 crash and has increased in intensity and enthusiasm ever since. After spending two years on the sidelines doing detailed observation and analysis, I took the plunge in 1970 and became an ardent supporter of, and participant in, the intensely logical and mathematical nature of *correct* Stock Exchange investment procedures. Of course the word 'correct' is to be stressed here, since it is the crux of the whole issue.

My first book on the use of quantitative investment procedures on the Stock Exchange, entitled *Winning on the JSE*, appeared in 1988. It went into its third printing only 13 months after it first appeared and has been prescribed by at least one South African university for the B Com (Honours) course. These facts make me confident that there are many prospective investors who can be made enthusiastic about correct Stock Exchange procedures, provided the strictly quantitative approaches I adopt are revealed to them.

1.2 Sorting the corn from the chaff

Many books have been written stressing the *random* nature of the price movements of shares listed on the boards of the Stock Exchange. Many masters degrees in commerce have been awarded to proponents of what is esoterically termed the 'Random Walk Movement' or the 'Monte Carlo Principle' in this regard.

I differ fundamently with these people: *I maintain that the Stock Exchange should never be viewed as a whole.* This crucial distinction between my outlook on this subject and that of the random walkers warrants detailed discussion.

There are some 800 different companies listed on the boards of the Johannesburg Stock Exchange. For very good quantitative mathematical reasons, the shares of some of these will definitely rise in price during the forthcoming year. Others, for equally good mathematical reasons, will definitely fall in price during the same period.

The first requirement of the successful investor on the Stock Exchange is that he be capable of distinguishing between these two very different categories of shares. I ask the reader to believe me when I state that it is possible to do just that. To accomplish this end I formulated the approach put forward in my first book, which proposes nine laws with which any industrial or financial share considered for purchase should comply. I will review these laws in considerable detail in this text, but for the moment I merely wish here to indicate that there are methods of sorting the corn from the chaff.

From the knowledge that there are 'good' shares on the Stock Exchange whose prices have a high probability of rising because they deserve to do so for quantitative reasons, as well as 'bad' shares whose prices will drop for equally deserving quantitative reasons, it follows immediately that to talk of the Stock Exchange as a whole is unacceptable mathematically. Hence my antagonism towards the random walk proponents.

1.3 Removing the element of gambling from Stock Exchange operation

It will be found that my nine laws are sufficiently strict that only a select minority of shares satisfy them. This feature effectively removes the element of gambling from the scene.

The intention behind *Winning on the JSE* was to enable prospective investors to enter Stock Exchange operations as quickly and simply as possible, in other words, to provide a ready 'hands-on' approach. *Many important aspects were either glossed over or omitted completely* to achieve this end. It must be realised that an intensive study such as that of the Stock Exchange is never commenced at the beginning; one normally starts about one third of the way up.

This new text gives detailed consideration to these previously disregarded matters, since my readers will now have been able to appreciate the prime aim of my earlier book. To summarise the aim of all of my books on this topic, correct Stock Exchange investment is most definitely not gambling, and in point of fact will be shown to involve highly erudite considerations.

1.4 Why invest on the Stock Exchange?

So far I have elevated this form of investment out of the gambling arena and indicated that it follows from, and definitely requires, quantitative and mathematical selection procedures. But this has still not answered the fundamental question: *Why invest on the Stock Exchange in the first place*?

The answer can be given very succinctly. The magnitude of our current *inflation rate* makes this form of investment imperative. Detailed discussion is necessary at this juncture.

You see, my father at least had the choice of investing or not investing on the Stock Exchange. He was accustomed, in the 1950s, to an inflation rate of some 3% to 4%. At that time 12 month fixed deposit interest rates with a building society yielded 8%. Let me now explain why he had no need to turn to Stock Exchange investments.

The figure quoted by a building society for its fixed deposit interest rate is a pre-tax figure. Let us assume that my father's average tax rate was 25%. Getting 8% pre-tax thus converts to an after-tax interest rate of three quarters of 8%, that is 6%. With inflation running at 3%, he was able to obtain what is esoterically termed a 'real' return on his fixed deposit investments of 6%-3%, or 3%. The word 'real' here means the after-tax interest rate minus the pertaining inflation rate. Thus persons investing in building society fixed deposits in the 1950s were quite definitely able to obtain a real interest rate of some 3% per annum.

No effort or worry was associated with such investment procedures. One merely went to the building society, chose the period for a fixed deposit which suited one's financial requirements, signed on the dotted line, and lo and behold, when the maturity date of that deposit dawned the investor had achieved a positive real interest rate. *The investor of the 1950s can be said to have been spoilt with regard to the ease with which the ideal of a real return on his capital could be achieved.* The crux was, of course, the relative magnitudes of the pretax investment rate and the pertaining inflation rate.

Things are diametrically opposite in the year 1989. I have proved in some ten articles in the financial press that the inflation rate of for example, a two offspring family paying off the bond on its home is approximately 30%. This topic is of such importance that the whole of chapter 2 is devoted to an in-depth discussion of the exact meaning of the phrase 'inflation rate' and the precise mathematical manner in which each individual family can calculate its own pertaining figure.

Chapter 2 shows that no two families will have the same inflation rate, since some will have bond-free homes, while others will still be paying off their bonds. Some families will have schoolgoing children, and others will have no children or their children will already have left home. The inflation rate for each such family will have its own characteristic figure. A knowledge of his own inflation rate is of vital importance to each householder, since ideally this should determine his investment plans and techniques. As stated briefly above, the aim is to achieve a real interest rate of a positive value.

I do not want to break the main line of thought at this point by paying too much attention to the intricacies and esoteric adjuncts of the phrase 'inflation rate'. All that is necessary at this stage of the text is the statement that most of the families that I know of will be experiencing an inflation rate of some 30%. Full details in support of this figure are given in chapter 2.

We turn, now, to a consideration of the avenues of investment capable of providing the investor with a real return on his funds under such circumstances. I can state quite honestly that, to the best of my knowledge, investing on the Stock Exchange provides the best manner of achieving this goal. I wish to go even further and say that *only through investment on the Stock Exchange can this requirement of a real return be provided*, but obviously I must stop short of such an unequivocal opinion, even though I sincerely believe it to be true.

To summarise, then, it is the magnitude of a typical South African family's inflation rate in the year 1989 that makes *correct* investment on the Stock Exchange *a virtually imperative technique*. The aim of this book is to indicate how this 'correct' method of investment is to be achieved.

There is one further aim of this text, namely to enable the investor to actually *enjoy* his sojourn on the Stock Exchange. I will attempt to alleviate, if not remove completely, any feelings of anxiety or worry that most people believe are the unavoidable concomitant of investing on the Stock Exchange. Apparently the current opinion is that one may resort to this method of investment provided that one has nerves of steel and a temperament to go with them. My goal here is to prove to my readers that it is possible, by following the methods of analysis proposed in this text, to enjoy investing on the Stock Exchange to such an extent that one *looks forward* to one's next purchase of suitable shares.

1.5 Investment on the Stock Exchange, approached correctly, builds character

To state that correct Stock Exchange investment actually builds character may seem very far-fetched. However, for the reasons discussed below, I assure the reader that it is indeed so.

The essence of correct Stock Exchange investment is that the investor has to *put his money where his brains are.* Doing so, and seeing his efforts reap the rewards they deserve if his analyses prove correct, greatly increases his confidence in his decision-making abilities. *Without fail, this causes his self-image to improve dramatically.*

Let me admit quite honestly that after nearly 20 years of participation on the Stock Exchange, I still gain a tremendous thrill when a share that I select for purchase, following detailed and lengthy analysis, at, say, 130 cents in the morning, closes at 140 cents that night. This exuberance relates only slightly to the monetary gain involved, and primarily to the fact that my analytic abilities proved to be competent. Only those who have actually experienced such a share price rise in one day will know what I am attempting to describe here.

I also admit, equally honestly, that after these 20 years the first page I turn to when reading the morning newspaper is that containing the closing Stock Exchange prices and the volume of sales that took place in each share. I still listen every evening to the closing Stock Exchange prices at 18h15. However, I state yet again that I do not do all this merely for the monetary gain involved. It is the feeling of *personal satisfaction* arising out of *deserved achievement* that is all-important. Let me explain the reason for this in more detail now.

Take the case of a person who wishes to purchase a shirt. At the shop of his choice there is normally a very wide choice of shirts from which to make his selection. He compares colours, styles, cuts and the like and may even actually try on his ultimate short list of selections prior to making his purchase. There are three crucial considerations of which the buyer is rarely aware. First, *he is not buying an article which has been rejected, and hence is no longer wanted, by its initial owner.* Second, there is a definite selling price which conventionally is not open to argument. Third, the buyer is not rushed in his prospective purchase in any way; he can go back the next day if he is uncertain and wishes to think things over at home, or even to compare the shirts available at another shop.

None of these three considerations applies in the case of the purchase of a share on the Stock Exchange. I will discuss this vital point in far greater detail later on in this text, but for the time being it is important that the reader not acquainted with it should appreciate its validity at this early stage.

First, and by far the most important point to appreciate with regard to operations on the Stock Exchange, the share the prospective buyer wishes to acquire can only be acquired because *it has been rejected by its present owner.* Hence the first way in which operation on the Stock Exchange builds character is by greatly developing the buyer's confidence in his decision-making ability.

I will indicate the steps involved in the purchase of a suitable share in great detail later in this text. For the moment let me summarise the process in order to make some very important observations.

According to my nine laws of Stock Exchange operation, the investor waits until either the interim or the preliminary financial results have appeared. Then he subjects the income statement and balance sheet to close quantitative scrutiny in accordance with the principles outlined in my laws. He performs certain important calculations to obtain certain quantitative information about the company he is analysing. Finally he comes to the bottom-line decision, which no one else can make for him, namely *is the share in question worthy of purchase*?

Even after 20 years' operation I still take some four hours to come to my final decision on this score. And when I have done so, I still write myself a letter detailing how and why I came to my final decision. All this after 20 years of ten hours' participation per normal working day!

Let us presume that the share in question has satisfied all of my nine laws, and thus is a candidate for purchase. I now have to come to grips with the realisation that in purchasing this share, I am obtaining it from a person who is so dissatisfied with it that he no longer wants to possess it. In other words, *my possession is the result of his rejection of the same goods.*

Now the ultimate question. Of the two of us, who is right? Obviously we cannot both be correct. *I want what he no longer wants.* This, very succinctly, is the essence of Stock Exchange entry.

This is where the attribute of confidence in one's quantitative abilities is either born or enhanced. The prospective investor must now put his money where his brains are. He cannot lean on anyone else; he is on his own.

One method of acquiring this degree of self-confidence is by *starting slowly.* Instead of purchasing, say, 1 000 shares at the outset, the newcomer may commence by buying only 100. If the share price rises in the following months (note: not days or weeks), he slowly but surely acquires that character trait most desirable in correct Stock Exchange participation, namely *confidence in his own decision-making capabilities.*

This, then, is the first way in which operation on the Stock Exchange builds character. There is another one, namely *rapid decision making.* This comes into play as follows.

I stated above that a person who wishes to purchase a shirt sees a fixed selling price marked on the article he intends to buy. This does not apply to the purchase of shares on the Stock Exchange. Let us assume that a prospective investor has finally decided that the share he has analysed is worthy of purchase. Obviously he has taken into account the last selling price of this share in arriving at this conclusion. Now he wishes to buy the share. But at what price? He must phone his stockbroker and give him *limits* on the purchase price. There may not be a seller at yesterday's closing price and the current sellers' price may well be some 10 to 15 cents more than the latter. In other words, there is no fixed selling price of a share as there is in the case of a shirt. It is a situation of bargaining, wherein the buyer indicates his desired acquisition price range and the seller attempts to increase this if possible.

This is where a prospective buyer must not only make up his mind, but also be able to do so in a hurry. There may well be other buyers equally enthusiastic about acquiring the very same shares. The investor does not have sole rights to the buying opportunity of his carefully selected share; there are other equally erudite persons on the scene.

Compare this situation with that of the person who wished to buy a shirt. He had a wide selection to choose from and ample time in which to make his decision. If the prospective share buyer does not act swiftly, he may lose out to other buyers, and if his initial offer of a purchase price is not well pitched, he may suffer the same fate. Thus a share purchaser is virtually always under pressure in attempting an equitable deal.

To summarise my outlook that correct Stock Exchange investment breeds character, we have, first, the finding that a quantitative decision as to whether or not to buy the share has to be made. Amongst others is the important consideration that the purchaser is acquiring what the seller is discarding. Only one of these two can be right; the other is horribly wrong. Second, the purchase price to be offered must take into account other possible buyers as well as the seller's figure. Third, more often than not these decisions have to be made in a hurry.

All in all, then, the purchaser's ability to make accurate decisions under pressure, with rather disastrous consequences should he be wrong, is considerably enhanced by correct Stock Exchange investment procedures. If he is right – and he has the protection of my nine laws in this connection to ensure a high probability of such an occurrence – the improvement in his self-image is so great that it has to be experienced personally to be described.

1.6 But what if the share price drops?

The above tacitly assumes that the price of a correctly chosen share will rise, and this fundamentally from the moment that the investor purchases it. Often this is the case, but equally often the share price drops after purchase. It has happened to me that some 30 minutes after my purchase at, say, 130 cents, the share price has actually dropped to 125 cents. Unless the explanation for such an apparently unhappy state of affairs is appreciated, the investor may well experience a sinking feeling in his stomach.

The reason for such an occurrence is simple to understand once the reader realises that not every shareholder in a company is well-informed. A shareholder who is not well-informed may also not realise the potential of the share he is attempting to sell. The fact that an investor has just completed his buying order when the former's selling order appears is merely unfortunate.

The seller may equally well have a need for the finances his selling order will provide him. He may have put in a swimming pool at his house, undergone renovations, bought a new car or have a hundred other similar reasons for requiring a considerable sum of finance at that time. Selling his shares merely provides him with the means to achieve his desired end.

Of course, a really confident investor who possesses additional finances will increase his previous share purchase by buying in this recently available quantity of shares at the lower price. Such action takes real confidence in one's abilities, but this will come as the success of the procedures to be employed is proven more and more often.

Here I am discussing a temporary drop in a share price. But what happens in a market crash, as occurred in October 1987? I will discuss this event in detail in chapter 9, but in the meantime let me answer the question briefly. My readers will understand *why* the crash occurred once they have read the chapter. At the time of such a crash he should not possess any overpriced shares if he has followed my laws. This is the important feature. His shares will drop in price, but conventionally not as drastically as those whose dramatically excessive prices were the initial cause of the crash. As I will point out via my own experiences in the October 1987 Stock Exchange crash, the prices of correctly chosen shares will rise again some one to two years later, and then will actually exceed their prices prior to the crash. During this time the investor still receives his dividend return, *since the company itself is in no way affected by Stock Exchange movements.*

This is an important point to realise. *The company whose shares have been purchased will continue its normal productive path, irrespective of the dramatic events on the Stock Exchange.* In so doing it will afford the investor who has chosen correctly his conventionally expected increase in dividend. And as a result, once investor confidence returns, as it inevitably must and will, the share price will recover its drop and will continue on its path as if nothing happened. To wait patiently and adopt the required frame of mind while all mayhem and devastation is going on around one is not easy to do, but achieved it can be with due experience.

1.7 Résumé

In this first chapter of this text I have attempted to convey to my readers many of my views on correct procedures of Stock Exchange investment. Acceptance and appreciation of these views are essential if the prime goal of the book, namely to make the reader actually *enjoy* his operations on the Stock Exchange, is to be achieved. There is to be no need to bite one's fingernails to the quick, to endure sleepless nights, or to have the apparently essential prerequisite for Stock Exchange operation of nerves of steel, and the final result need not be grey hair.

My first message in this regard is that correct Stock Exchange operation is most definitely *not* gambling. The second is that it is actually a highly erudite procedure, commencing on every occasion with a mathematical scrutiny of the income statement and balance sheet of the company whose shares are considered for purchase. My third message is that operation according to these principles cultivates certain desirable traits in the investor, the first being an enhanced ability to make decisions in general, the second the ability to make decisions quickly, and the third reinforced feelings of self-confidence should the price of the share chosen fall below its purchase price at some stage.

The rewards for using correct analytical skills are great indeed. First, obviously, is the monetary gain involved, and second, and possibly of even greater importance, is the improved self-image attained by a successful investor.

2

Each family must calculate its own inflation rate

Page

2.1 Introduction

As I indicated in chapter 1, the quantity against which each investor must measure the overall return he requires of his investments is termed the 'inflation rate'. To be even more precise, it is *his own specific value of his family's inflation rate* as opposed to that widely used, but amorphous (as I will show in this chapter) concept 'the South African inflation rate'.

This latter value is calculated each month by the government institution called Central Statistical Services. In the Johannesburg daily financial newspaper *Business Day* of 26 January 1989 I published my two mathematical reasons for what I allege were errors in procedure in the performance of this calculation by Central Statistical Services (CSS).

Possibly the best manner of commencing this chapter is by quoting directly from this article. It was headed: 'Take government's inflation rate – then double it!'

2.2 My mathematical reasons for discrediting CSS' procedure

The following is a direct quote from my article.

> Government's Central Statistical Services stated this week that the inflation rate for December, as measured by the change in the Consumer Price Index, was 12,5%. On the basis of applied mathematics I maintain it is 24% or higher.
>
> The Statistical News Release for November 1988 puts the annual rate of increase in the price index for food at 12,2%, and says this is the first time since March 1986 that this rate has been below the overall inflation rate.
>
> Unless employees of CSS in Pretoria enjoy special food prices, the procedure used to arrive at their conclusions warrants close scrutiny.
>
> The calculation of the postulated inflation rate figure is to me an applied mathematical procedure, not a statistical exercise or an economic project.
>
> Every research student knows that the first step in such a procedure is to offer a mathematical model of the situation being analysed. The accuracy of the final postulate rests in the first instance on the accuracy of the mathematical model.
>
> Unless I am mistaken, CSS has violated this most sacred of all sacred mathematical procedures in that they offer no mathematical model for their calculation of South Africa's inflation rate.
>
> In analogous terms, this is equivalent to building a high and architecturally intricate wall on flimsy foundations which are not readily available for inspection.
>
> The attitude of CSS just does not, in my own experience, agree with experimental fact. Thus began my mathematical enquiry into what CSS were doing to arrive at their postulated version of our inflation rate.
>
> Copi's text on *Introduction to Logic* states: 'A problem will not be felt by anyone who is ignorant of the accepted theories. One must be familiar with current theories, observant of new facts and uncomfortable in the presence of any conflict between fact and theory.'
>
> The inflation rate is not a factual figure. It is a postulate which emerges from numerous assumptions.

> I refuse to believe that everyone at CSS working on our inflation rate is completely comfortable in the presence of the conflict between their postulate and observed fact.
>
> It is stated by CSS that 22,72% of monthly disposable income is spent on food. There follows a detailed breakdown, including grain products at 3,33%; meat 7,71%; milk, cheese, eggs 2,16%; vegetables 2,45%; fruit and nuts 1,49%; and so on until the complete 22,72% figure is realised.
>
> As an applied mathematician I immediately stop in my reading tracks. CSS is offering us figures to the second decimal place. The amount spent on fruit and nuts is 1,49%. CSS is offering us an accuracy of one part in 149, that is of 0,67%. And this for a so-called average family.
>
> I asked one of their staff who is occupied with this topic how many children were postulated in this average family. I was stunned by the reply: they did not work on this basis. *They merely worked on the figures revealed in the thousands of questionnaires they send out.*
>
> Unless I am mistaken, herein lies the error. In any attempted mathematical analysis the postulated model of the situation must at the outset be stated in definitive terms. Whatever detailed calculations then follow must inevitably be judged solely and conclusively on the accuracy, feasibility, stability and the like of the postulated mathematical model.
>
> Yet CSS does not offer us its model of the family on which it is to place its extremely detailed breakdown of monthly disposable income.

I reproduce this extract from my article in its original form, as I am not in a position to improve upon my sentiments expressed therein regarding CSS' mathematical errors. My opinions were open to criticism or possible correction from a wide professional reading public.

However, the only criticism I received was in a letter from the Director of CSS which appeared in the *Business Day* of 27 January 1989, that is the day after my article was published. The letter described my article as a diatribe. In all my years at university I had never once used this word and I had to resort to a dictionary to discover its meaning. Letters appeared calling for an inflation debate on the South African Broadcasting Corporation's television services. Such a debate, for which I was completely prepared, never materialised.

A letter of congratulation which I still cherish was one from 'Pinched' of Greenside, Johannesburg. It appeared in the *Business Day* of 6 February 1989 and reads as follows:

> My congratulations on Karl Posel's article entitled 'Take Government's inflation rate – then double it'. This incisive article confirms what my cheque book and credit card have been telling me for months. His threefold proof certainly convinced me. I do hope that the civil servants in the CSS take note. Many thanks and my congratulations to the author.

2.3 A detailed analysis of my three mathematical family models

Following on the above I published a detailed analysis of my methods in the *Sunday Star* of 7 May 1989. Herein I considered in mathematical detail three completely different models of a South African family. Please note that these are *not* model families, as often appeared in print thereafter; they are family models, that is mathematical models of three different types of families.

I repeat this analysis here. The method used is actually very simple when viewed from a mathematical standpoint and I set out the required method step-by-step.

2.4 My first family model: two pre-teenage children and a home mortgage bond

As my first model of a typical South African family, I considered the instance where there are two pre-teenage children, an unemployed wife, a husband in middle management or the equivalent occupation, and a mortgage bond on the family home. This cannot be criticised for not actually existing or being feasible.

The very first step, now, is to tabulate the breakdown of monthly expenditure as it exists at the time of analysis, that is May 1989.

First that all-important item, expenditure on food. After a really intensive campaign of detailed questioning I came to the monthly figures of R400 per adult and R200 per child as a realistic expenditure. For the family under scrutiny, food absorbs R1 200 per month.

Second is the item bond repayments. It appears that R700 is an accurate estimate of the type of home and personal financing capabilities this type of family would enjoy.

Third is monthly expenditure on cars and transport. It is likely that there are two cars in the family, only one of which is fully paid for. I assume that the second car is relatively new and is being paid off at the rate of R500 per month. Expenditure on petrol is assumed to be R250 per month.

And so we proceed with the remaining items of conventional monthly expenditure. I ask the reader to note at the very outset the use of the word *expenditure* here. It may seem an obvious notion at this juncture, since after all what else can it be? Some economists have other ideas on this basic aspect, as I show later!

Figure 2.1 shows the detailed compilation required. Should the reader have other ideas regarding his own specific modes of expenditure, he should compile his own relevant table.

Figure 2.1 The details of monthly expenditure for model one of a typical South African family

Item of monthly expenditure	*Amount spent*	*Weighting factor %*	*Year-on-year % increase*	*Contribution to final inflation rate figure*
Food and household supplies	R1 200	32,4%	30	0,324 × 30 = 9,72%
Bond repayment	700	18,9%	50	0,189 × 50 = 9,45%
Car repayment	500	13,5%	20	0,135 × 20 = 2,70%
Petrol	250	6,75%	25	0,0675 × 25 = 1,69%
Car repairs	100	2,7%	50	0,027 × 50 = 1,35%
Education	50	1,35%	20	0,0135 × 20 = 0,27%
Chemist, personal care	150	4,05%	20	0,0405 × 20 = 0,81%
Electricity and water	150	4,05%	10	0,0405 × 10 = 0,41%
Domestic servant	150	4,05%	10	0,0405 × 10 = 0,41%
Clothes and footwear	150	4,05%	30	0,0405 × 30 = 1,22%
Telephone and TV	90	2,4%	20	0,024 × 20 = 0,48%
Entertainment	90	2,4%	40	0,024 × 40 = 0,96%
Sundries	120	3,2%	10	0,032 × 10 = 0,32%
TOTAL	R3 700	100,0%		Inflation rate: 29,79%

2.5 Step two: determining the weighting factors

The second step is to determine what are esoterically termed the weighting factors. *These are merely the proportion which each of the items shown in figure 2.1 contributes towards total monthly expenditure.*

For example, taking the item food, we see that it contributes R1 200 of a total monthly expenditure of R3 700. Thus the weighting factor is 1 200/3 700, that is 0,324 or 32,4%. The remaining factors are as shown in figure 2.1.

2.6 Step three: the year-on-year percentage increases

Steps one and two are simple in that they pertain to conditions presently experienced. Step three is more difficult in that information about conditions prevailing exactly one year previously are required. Thus, for example, with regard to monthly expenditure on food, we need to know the percentage increase in the current amount *over that of one year previously*.

People who use credit cards for supermarket and similar store purchases will have ready access to accurate figures. A second method which is useful for non-credit card shoppers is to look at food advertisements in year-old newspapers.

Whatever the case, a person who wishes to calculate his own inflation rate needs to obtain accurate information about the year-on-year percentage increases pertaining to each of the items of expenditure detailed in the table in figure 2.1. In figure 2.1 I provide information offered to me by willing participants.

2.7 Step four: the multiplication process

For mathematical reasons which need not occupy us now, for each item of expenditure in the table in figure 2.1, the weighting factor must be multiplied by the percentage year-on-year increase as shown. Thus, for example, with regard to the food item, the weighting factor of 32,4%, or 0,324 must be multiplied by the 30% year-on-year increase in this item to yield the figure of 9,72%, as shown.

2.8 The final step: adding all these amounts

The final step is to add all the amounts resulting from the above multiplication procedure. *The result is the inflation rate pertaining, please note, specifically and only to the family model under analysis.*

The emergent figure is 29,79%, which stands in sharp contrast to CSS' hopefully optimistic figure of some 15%.

In further contradiction to the figure calculated by CSS, we see that in figure 2.1 the contributions of the items food, bond repayments and transport *on their own* result in the amount of 9,72 + 9,45 + 2,7 + 1,69 + 1,35, or 24,91%. How on earth can CSS be confident of its postulate of an inflation rate as low as 15%?

2.9 Model two of a typical South African family

Not every South African family has a mortgage bond on its home. Many will have paid off this loan already and hence must be analysed differently. This is the situation of my model two family.

I go one step further. It is most likely that the mortgage bond will have been liquidated in a family in which the parents are some twenty years older than those in model one. Therefore it is probable that one of the two offspring attends university. This latter fact has far-reaching effects.

From what I have been able to observe of this one-offspring-at-university family, three cars feature. The third is a real 'banger', conventionally either Dad's or Mom's previous model which somehow or other is still capable of commuting daily to and from campus. The petrol and repair bills increase accordingly, and the final result I postulate will look something like what is indicated in the table in figure 2.2. The comparable increases over items in figure 2.1 should be noted.

Figure 2.2 The details of monthly expenditure for model two family: the bond has been liquidated and one of the offspring is at University

Item of monthly expenditure	*Amount spent*	*Weighting factor %*	*Year-on-year % increase*	*Contribution to final inflation rate figure*
Food: in house	R1 200	32,1	30	0,321 × 30 = 9,63%
ex house	150	4,0	60	0,04 × 60 = 2,40%
Car repayment	500	13,4	20	0,134 × 20 = 2,68%
Petrol	300	8,0	25	0,08 × 25 = 2,00%
Car repairs	200	5,3	50	0,053 × 50 = 2,65%
Education: fees	300	8,0	30	0,08 × 30 = 2,40%
books	100	2,7	60	0,027 × 60 = 1,62%
Chemist, personal care	250	6,7	20	0,067 × 20 = 1,34%
Electricity and water	150	4,0	10	0,04 × 10 = 0,4%
Domestic servant	150	4,0	10	0,04 × 10 = 0,4%
Clothes and footwear	200	5,3	30	0,053 × 30 = 1,59%
Telephone and TV	120	3,2	20	0,032 × 20 = 0,64%
Entertainment	120	3,2	40	0,032 × 40 = 1,28%
TOTAL	R3 740	100,0%		Inflation rate: 29,03%

Despite widely differing amounts and types of expenditure, in this instance compared with the two pre-teenage children and bond-repaying model one South African family, we see that *the final inflation rate figure for our model two family – 29,03% – is remarkably close to the figure of 29,79% derived for model one.*

Once again it must be pointed out that the figure postulated by CSS – 15% – looks rather ridiculous.

2.10 Model three: the retired couple

The calculation of the inflation rate of a retired family unit is an extremely interesting investigation.

There appear to be three types of such a family. In the first, the retired couple lives in its own home, now completely bond-free. In the second, the couple lives in a retirement village, and in the third, the retired couple lives with one of its children. Here I analyse only the first of these options.

From talks with such a couple it appears that certain salient differences arise compared with the previous family models. *First, the disposable income is definitely constrained to a fixed sum.* I will assume the after-tax figure of R2 000 a month as a typical amount achieved through careful pre-retirement financial planning.

Second, it would appear that such a couple plans to spend all of this figure each month, since considerations of saving for old age have now vanished. Having reached old age, the couple intends to enjoy this time to the full.

For security reasons, conventionally two large dogs feature in the life of our retired couple. Food and veterinary services average out at R100 per month, with an annual year-on-year increase of 50% in the latter.

The fourth surprising aspect to some is the relatively large sum spent monthly on hobbies. With the time now at its disposal, the retired couple, I am informed, devotes at least four hours per day to hobbies such as woodwork, tapestry, knitting and the like. The monthly bill for this is typically R100, with a 50% year-on-year increase pertaining.

Food remains at R400 per person, with entertainment increasing to spend such funds as might remain. Afternoon cinemas, eating out at reasonable prices, entertaining grandchildren and the like amount to some R100 monthly.

Expenditure on reading material increases. The sum of a R100 month is typical, with a year-on-year increase of 60%. Petrol costs R200 per month because of the many pleasurable excursions now being undertaken.

Using the above information, the table in figure 2.3 can be compiled.

Figure 2.3 The third mathematical family model: the retired couple

Item of monthly expenditure	*Amount spent*	*Weighting factor %*	*Year-on-year % increase*	*Contribution to final inflation rate figure*
Food	R800	40	30	0,4 × 30 = 12,0%
Petrol	200	10	25	0,1 × 25 = 2,5%
Dogs	100	5	50	0,05 × 50 = 2,5%
Medical fees	100	5	20	0,05 × 20 = 1,0%
Medical drugs	100	5	60	0,05 × 60 = 3,0%
Hobbies, etc	100	5	50	0,05 × 50 = 2,5%
Entertainment	100	5	30	0,05 × 30 = 1,5%
Electricity and water	100	5	10	0,05 × 10 = 0,5%
Telephone and TV	100	5	20	0,05 × 60 = 3,0%
Books, etc	100	5	60	0,05 × 20 = 1,0%
Chemist, personal care	100	5	20	0,05 × 20 = 1,0%
Sundries	100	5	10	0,05 × 10 = 0,5%
TOTAL	R2 000	100%		Inflation rate: 31,0%

Once again, despite completely different amounts of expenditure, the final inflation rate of the retired couple as analysed emerges as 31%, a figure remarkably close to the 29% of the previous two models.

2.11 What is meant by 'the South African inflation rate'?

For some time now I have puzzled over the precise mathematical meaning of the concept '*the* South African inflation rate'. As a mere mathematician, I am able to grasp only the notion of definitive models to which equally definitive inflation rates apply after close analysis.

Be that as it may, what is of importance to the investor is his own inflation rate figure. At present I just cannot see a figure for this far removed from 30%, and it is for this reason that I use it in chapter 1.

2.12 Repercussions of my calculations of the inflation rate

The reader who merely wanted the quantitative manner in which I arrived at the inflation rate of some 30% for a typical South African family can omit the rest of this chapter. However, for the more enthusiastic reader, who might be interested in the repercussions of my two articles mentioned earlier, I offer the consequential occurrences. After all, one does not indicate lightly that an august government institution has committed esoteric mathematical errors in their calculations, particularly when the topic under analysis is one as important as that of the inflation rate of a typical South African family with all its investment repercussions.

Never before in my professional career have I had a complete newspaper editorial devoted to one of my scientific findings. Now, for the first time, not one but two complete editorials in the Durban newspaper the *Natal Mercury* were devoted to my findings on the mathematical calculation of the correct inflation rate.

The editorial reproduced in figure 2.4 appeared on 13 February 1989. It is reproduced in full in its original form so that my readers may do an in-depth appraisal of its content. The inflation rate and the calculation thereof by means of acceptable mathematical concepts of *a priori* models gathered great interest.

On 10 May 1989, in response to my detailed article in the *Sunday Star* of 7 May, the editorial reproduced in figure 2.5 appeared. Any readers who may have harboured some doubts as to the scientific validity of my inflation rate calculations will appreciate the comments contained therein.

2.13 Resolving a subtle and highly esoteric mathematical argument

The argument in question is an esoteric one, although it may be resolved relatively simply, concerning the topics prices, on the one hand, and

Figure 2.4 Natal Mercury Editorial: The Posel Factor

The Natal Mercury

THE POSEL FACTOR

HOUSEWIVES will hardly need to concern themselves with the calculations Professor Karl Posel, a former professor of applied mathematics, used to conclude that South Africa's real rate of inflation is about double what the Government's Central Statistical Services (CSS) say it is. Most shoppers would say their monthly food bills confirm the professor's sums.

His challenge is based on the charge that CSS do not offer a valid mathematical model of the situation being analysed.

Taking a typical middle-income family, Prof Posel says it spends much more on food, for example, than the 22,72% of disposable income that CSS allocate. He also finds that the price of groceries rises 10% every three months – a much higher rate than CSS give.

Other empirical evidence, he says, confirms that the real over-all inflation rate is closer to 26% than the official figure of 12-13%. He also cites 17 items, including milk, bread, cars, tyres, paint and shoes, that have doubled in price in three years – an annual increase of 26%.

CSS, of course, insist that their consumer price index is an accurate measure of the inflation rate and dismiss the professor's arguments as 'a diatribe'.

We don't know who is right. But what we do know is that one of the established facts of economic life that holds good at all times and in all places is that over a period of time there is a close correlation between the rise in money supply and the general rise in consumer prices. Recent computer models have confirmed that this is also true in South Africa.

In 1986, after years of uncontrolled and wildly erratic growth in money supply, the Government introduced a target range for the expansion of M3, as it is known. Last year the target range was between 12% and 16%. Discounting real economic growth at a maximum of 2%, this predicts an inflation rate of between 10% and 14%, after lags and blips in the graph have been ironed out.

That is bad enough. But the really bad news is that the Government overshot its 16% target by a whopping 10%. In the peak month of November it pumped 27,7% more cash and credit into the system than the previous November.

Again discounting a generous 2% for the country's real increase in wealth, we are left with a monetary inflation rate that is so close to Prof Posel's 26% as makes no difference.

We still don't know who is right. But unless the Government sets, and strictly adheres to a realistic money growth target (the closer to zero the better), we would bet our devalued Mickey Mouse rands on Prof Posel.

Figure 2.5 Natal Mercury Editorial: Still on Autopilot

The Natal Mercury

STILL ON AUTOPILOT

WITH INTEREST rates soaring, domestic savings near rock-bottom, unbridled government spending, wildly erratic money supply and chronic inflation, many South Africans feel they are like passengers on an aircraft flying through a storm towards an uncertain destination.

The economically literate among them know that the aircraft is inherently strong, airworthy, and capable of a safe landing. If it were not, it could not have withstood the fierce buffeting it has taken, including some R13 000 million in foreign debt repayments since 1985.

Up on the flight deck, however, all is not well. Since Mr PW Botha's failure to cross the Rubicon of political reform in 1985, the economy has been more or less on autopilot. And for much longer than that, the Treasury was flying blind on money supply. Now it has target ranges, though they mean little. When the politicians want money, they get it.

But in spite of the turbulence it was generally assumed that the compass was working and the maps and measuring instruments were accurate.

Now it seems we may be deprived of even that comfort. Some weeks ago Dr Karl Posel, a former professor of applied mathematics who also knows his way round the stock exchange, challenged the accuracy of the Government's official consumer price index. The true rate of increase, he claimed, was closer to 31% a year than the 14% put out by Central Statistical Services. Many housewives, trolley for trolley, as the saying goes, would agree with him.

CSS stoutly defends the accuracy of its figures. But Dr Posel's cry has been taken up by others, notably the Shareholders' Assocation, which rightly holds that the official index is 'critical to the performance of public listed companies'. Its initial survey of actual store prices of about 100 household items tends to confirm Dr Posel's figure of 31%.

Mr Harry Schwarz, MP, has called for an immediate scientific investigation of Dr Posel's claims. This is imperative. The CPI is one of our most important economic indicators. It is the yardstick by which inflation is usually measured, although it is not the disease itself – merely a symptom.

The disease is the excessive creation of money, and only the Government has the power to order that – or stop it. Over long periods the rise in consumer prices closely follows the increase in excess money.

An analysis of the average rate of increase in money supply would therefore be an important part of the investigation, and should provide a check on Dr Posel's claim. Monetarists could be forgiven a wry smile of satisfaction if the figures tended to confirm his theory.

expenditure, on the other, in the matter of the calculation of the inflation rate.

I have received a letter from an economist who cannot understand what the fuss is all about. 'Surely', he writes, 'all that need be done is to obtain the price of a basket of commodities pertaining in May 1989 and compare the price of the same basket pertaining precisely one year earlier'. After all, this is what he was taught in his economics course at university.

Unfortunately, there is a horrible, fundamental error of mathematical principle herein. The error in the basket of commodities approach is so subtle that I will proceed very slowly with the argument.

The idea is to take a trolley full of commodities in May 1989, total up the price involved, and find the total cost of the same trolley one year previously. It sounds so simple that the reader may possibly be wondering what the fuss is all about. We proceed with prices for May 1989 obtained from a survey done by the *Sunday Star* of 28 May 1989.

Product	*May 1989*	*May 1988*	*% Change*
Milk, 1ℓ	R 1,35	R 0,92	
Bread, 1 loaf	0,76	0,65	
Washing powder, 1 × 1kg packet	2,69	1,86	
Cut corn, 1 × 1kg packet	4,99	3,45	
Frozen chicken, per kg	3,99	2,79	
Ricoffy, 1 × 750g tin	6,44	5,49	
Peanut butter, 1 × 410g jar	2,19	1,85	
Sugar, 1 × 2,5kg packet	3,19	2,99	
Coke, 1 × 2ℓ bottle	2,89	1,55	
Toothpaste, 1 tube	1,85	1,69	
Shampoo, 1 × 350ml bottle	2,19	1,85	
	32,53	25,09	+29,7%
Milk powder, 1 × 5kg packet	33,00	31,00	
	R65,53	R56,09	+16,8%

Obviously I could extend this list, but it is sufficient as it is to make the required point. I wonder if the reader has already ascertained the error of principle I am alluding to. *It centres about the digit '1' in the above columns*, which digit I have been very careful to accentuate.

In other words, the economist's trolley, or basket as he prefers to call it, of the foodstuffs shown contains only *one of each of the items specified* – one litre of milk, one loaf of bread, one packet of washing powder, and so on down the line.

But now let us think in terms of actual *consumption per month*, which leads directly to actual *expenditure on food per month, as our tables in figures 2.1, 2.2 and 2.3 require.*

If we were to fill a trolley on the basis of monthly consumption, which is the correct approach to take, in all likelihood we would have the following quantities for my first family model of two pre-teenage children.

Product	*Quantity*	*Cost:May 1989*	*Cost:May 1988*	*% Change*
Milk	90ℓ	R121,50	R 82,80	
Bread	60 loaves	45,60	39,00	
Washing powder	1 packet	2,69	1,86	
Cut corn	5 packets	24,95	17,25	
Frozen chickens	12 kg	47,88	33,48	
Ricoffy	1 tin	6,44	5,49	
Peanut butter	2 jars	4,38	3,70	
Sugar	2×2,5kg packets	6,38	5,98	
Coke	15×2ℓ bottles	43,35	23,25	
Toothpaste	2 tubes	3,70	3,38	
Shampoo	2 bottles	4,38	3,70	
		R311,25	R219,89	+41,5%
Milk powder	½×5kg packet	16,50	15,50	
		R327,75	235,39	+39,2%

Let me make my point without considering the item milk powder.

On the economist's concept of a trolley of foodstuffs, whereby he tacitly and automatically takes *one of each item*, the total cost of the trolley shown in May 1989, R32,53, is 29,7% more than the cost of the same trolley in May 1988, R25,09.

However, disregarding this 'one of each' trolley and considering instead the mathematical requirement of the actual number of items consumed per month, we see that for the identical brand names the total cost of our consumption trolley in May 1989, R311,25, is 41,5% greater than the cost of the same trolley in May 1988, R219,89. Hence the great difference in percentage increases.

Thus the first mathematical error in the economist's trolley – a single item of each foodstuff – is only too obvious. There is another error, which I call the 'swamping error', and which is discussed in 2.14.

2.14 The swamping error

Consider, now, the presence of the 5kg packet of milk powder which I show separately in the above tables.

The concept of a swamping error arises when one item is priced at approximately that of some twenty or more other individual items. Thus, for example, the 5kg packet of milk powder at the May 1989 price of R33 completely swamps the R32,53 cost of the numerous other items shown.

If the year-on-year percentage increase in price of this swamping item also happens to be far less than that experienced for the other items, as actually was the case with milk powder, a completely distorted picture is obtained. On the economist's single item trolley concept, there is a 16,8% year-on-year price increase. If, on the other hand, we revert to the mathematically correct consumption trolley, we see a 39,2% year-on-year increase, since the swamping item is required in only a small quantity.

In other words, mathematical rigour and logic are required in each analysis.

2.15 In conclusion

The economist obtains his figure for the inflation rate by means of what is esoterically termed the *consumer price index*. In this chapter I show in detail that this is a mathematical misnomer. Instead, it should be the *consumer expenditure index*. There is a world of difference between these two topics.

3

Selecting an industrial share: from the very beginning

Page

3.1 Introduction

In the previous chapters I have *told* the reader a great deal about correct Stock Exchange investment procedures. Among the topics covered were character enhancement due to rapid decision making and gains in confidence and improvements in self-image if decisions prove to be correct. Now it is time to *show* the reader, utilising a 'hands on' approach, how to go about investing on the Stock Exchange. As the well-known song from the Broadway hit 'My Fair Lady' says – 'Don't Tell Me; Show Me!'.

The derivation and explanation of the fundamental concepts earnings-per-share, dividend and dividend yield, price-earnings ratio and earnings yield, and the interpretation and analysis of an income statement and balance sheet are covered in great detail in my first book, *Winning on the JSE*, and therefore there is no need to repeat all of this here. Thus, in what follows I assume that my readers are well acquainted with this essential background.

What I will repeat here, however, is the aim and content of my fundamental nine laws, with which any share considered for purchase should comply. My starting point is the very beginning – the process of selecting a suitable industrial share. In fact, I shall commence at a point even more fundamental than my point of departure in my first book, in that I will give consideration to the *tax implications* of an investor's Stock Exchange activities.

In 1.3 I stated that my first book either glossed over or completely omitted certain important aspects of investing on the Stock Exchange. This was done to provide my readers with the simplest and quickest possible hands-on approach to the purchase of suitable shares. The omission of possibly the greatest importance was the tax implications of an investor's activities on the Stock Exchange, and this gap will be filled in great detail in later chapters of this text. As he proceeds the reader will appreciate the reasons for the absence of this topic in the earlier and simpler text; tax arguments can become so involved and so intricate that only someone who has already become a Stock Exchange investor is in a position to understand all the innuendoes which can and do arise. It is to lead the reader slowly and carefully into this complex, yet economically vital topic that I address these tax considerations at this early stage of this book.

To present the cardinal point of these tax considerations at the very outset, it is to be able to persuade Inland Revenue that the investor has purchased his shares as what are esoterically termed 'capital assets' as opposed to 'revenue assets' or 'stock in trade'. The tax advantages awarded to the former classification are so great that many an advocate has been able to put his offspring through University and enjoy overseas holidays from the proceeds of his law practice if his clients have claimed the capital asset definition, only to find that Inland Revenue has bitterly opposed them with the opposite revenue asset assertion.

At this early stage let me reveal to my readers a vital aspect of South African Tax law; fundamentally *the taxpayer is guilty until proved innocent*. This is no exaggeration, and my readers will realise the stringency of the situation upon appreciating that in every other aspect of the law, *a person is innocent until proved guilty*.

Thus, although my readers may not yet be in a position to fully appreciate the important implications hereof, the fundamental aim of all *investors* on the Stock Exchange will be to make any share purchases in such a manner that they are able at all times to persuade Inland Revenue that the deals were done in order to acquire *capital assets* and not *stock in trade*. Precisely how to achieve this is dealt with in considerable detail below. This crucial aspect is mentioned now because the reader must be acquainted with it for his future assessments or analyses of shares he considers to be possible candidates for purchase.

3.2 Obtaining a real return on finances invested

As mentioned in 1.4, the aim of an investor is always to obtain what is termed a 'real return' on his finances. The phrase real return means that the after-tax return on investments minus the ruling value of the inflation rate results in a positive quantity.

Now consider specifically the case of investment in shares listed on the Stock Exchange. Before we consider the *after-tax* return obtained, we have to obtain the *pre-tax* return. In Stock Exchange operations this pre-tax return is made up of two completely separate components, dealt with individually below.

The first component of the pre-tax return is the *dividend yield*. The total amount of dividends the investor receives during the period of one year from the date of purchase of the share in question, divided by the purchase price, gives the component of his investment return provided by the dividends accrued. This is termed the 'dividend yield'. If the shares are purchased according to the methods advocated in this text, the dividend yield will be of the order of some 9% to 12%.

The Stock Exchange investor of conventional means will be allowed one third of this dividend yield as tax exempt. This means that his after-tax return from his dividend yield will range from some 6%, being two thirds of 9%, to 8%, being two thirds of 12%.*

However, chapter 2 indicates that at the time of writing this text (July 1989), a typical South African family has an inflation rate of some 30%. If his after-tax dividend return is only 8%, *how does a Stock Exchange investor manage to obtain a real return on his finances invested*?

The answer is given by the second and more important component of the total return on his shares. This component is the *increase in his share price one year after its purchase*.

A numerical example is helpful at this point. Let us assume that an investor pays 100 cents for his share. The actual number of shares purchased does not enter into the argument at all, for reasons to be seen shortly. Let the dividend received per share over the next year be 12 cents. This means that his pre-tax dividend return is 12/100 or 12%, and his after-tax dividend return two thirds of this 12%, or 8%.

Over this period of one year let the share price increase from the 100 cents at purchase to 140 cents. This is a typical order of magnitude which I expect. The investor's return from the share price increase, which is termed the 'capital appreciation', is 40%. This is a pre-tax return.

Now for the very essence of correct Stock Exchange investment. If the investor has complied with all of Inland Revenue's requirements to have his share purchase classified as *the acquisition of a capital asset*, the capital appreciation due to the increase in share price *is completely exempt from tax*. This means that the after-tax return from this component is the same as its pre-tax magnitude, namely 40%.

The total after-tax return achieved by the Stock Exchange investor is 48%, being the sum of the 8% dividend yield and the 40% capital appreciation. Since inflation is running at 30% per annum, the investor has achieved a 48% – 30%, or 18%, real return on his invested finances.

My readers are probably already asking how to comply with Inland Revenue's requirements so as to obtain the classification 'capital asset' for their shares. There are many facets to this topic, but for the time

---

* As of 14 March 1990, all three thirds of dividend income are tax free.

being the most important is that the share purchased should have what is classified as a *high dividend yield*. That is, it should be of the order of some 8% minimum, and not the 2% figure of many of what are termed 'blue chip' shares. A high dividend yield at the time of purchase is possibly the simplest way of convincing Inland Revenue that a participant on the Stock Exchange falls into the desirable category 'investors' rather than the ignominious group 'speculators'. More on this important aspect in later chapters.

3.3 How does an investor ensure an increase in his share price?

I have shown that the essential element to obtain a real return on invested finances is *an adequate increase in the share price* over one year. How does an investor ensure the successful accomplishment of this goal?

In other words, a Stock Exchange participant purchasing his selected share *now*, wishes to ensure that in *one year's time* his share price will have increased suitably. How does he go about achieving this?

Obviously, such an achievement cannot be guaranteed. At best, an investor can adopt a procedure which has a high probability of success in this regard. One such procedure, which I recommend, is scrutiny of a share in terms of my nine laws with which any share ultimately selected for purchase should comply. This leads me to the enunciation of my first law:

> ***Law 1:*** *If the prospective investor does not know precisely what he is doing, then the Stock Exchange is no place to be doing it.*

3.4 Eliminating a major risk factor by timing a share purchase correctly

My second law is intended to eliminate one of the major risk factors in Stock Exchange operation, namely the *timing* of the purchase of shares. This law has been considered to be extremely stringent by some reviewers of my first book, but I would advise any prospective investor to obey it to the letter.

A newcomer to the Stock Exchange may justifiably feel that he is at liberty to purchase his chosen shares at any time during the year. Obviously I am not intent on limiting his freedom in this regard; my aim is to save him from a predicament which in the past has befallen many an unwary operator. On the basis of my extremely detailed observation, over many years, of the workings of the Stock Exchange, I propose that *a share be purchased on only two occasions during its financial year*, namely immediately *after* the appearance of its interim (that is six months into the financial year) results, or immediately *after* the appearance of its preliminary (that is after the full year) results. On no other occasion should a share be purchased. Thus my second law:

> ***Law 2:*** *Purchase only after the publication of the company's financial results, either interim or preliminary.*

What I aim to achieve with this law is to make sure that concrete quantitative information about the company's performance is obtained *before* any decision regarding the possible purchase of its shares is contemplated. By waiting for the publication of its *most recent* results, a Stock Exchange investor is obtaining the *latest financial information* regarding that company.

Since correct Stock Exchange operation is based on a really onerous task, namely being able to predict events one year ahead, surely such prediction should commence from solid and rock-firm fundamentals which are beyond all suspicion and conjecture? What better means of achieving this extremely difficult aim than the most recent financial results?

The application of my second law has saved me from financial disaster on many occasions by restricting my choice of what I had regarded as suitable shares. How often has the reader seen in the financial press that a particular company is bound to come up with really fantastic results, only to find when these results finally appear that it performed really dismally due to completely unforeseen circumstances?

If the share in question commences its price rise some one to two weeks before the release of its financial results, I am still completely prepared to forego this portion of my possible capital appreciation in order to obtain enhanced security by waiting for the ultimate publication. If that share is worthy of purchase, *its price will still increase substantially after the official release of its results.*

I cannot adequately impress my standpoint on this crucial issue upon the prospective Stock Exchange investor. *It is far better to obtain a 40% share price increase with a high degree of certainty than an 80% increase shrouded in doubt and risk.*

This, then, is the starting point of my attempts to get the prospective investor to actually enjoy his operations on the Stock Exchange. One always commences with an attitude of relative certainty, and not of risk.

Therefore, although the temptation may often be very great, purchase a share on only two occasions during its financial year. Both of these occasions are related to the publication of its financial results.

3.5 Eliminating further risk factors: the financial pedigree of a share

Enjoyment of Stock Exchange participation can occur only if the risk factors are minimised or eliminated completely. Law 1 requests a certain degree of knowledge from the prospective investor and Law 2 insists on the correct timing of a share purchase. Thus these two laws concern what may be termed the *modus operandi*, that is the method or procedure.

The remaining seven laws concern the share itself, specifically the new concept of its *financial pedigree*.

Since it is of such vital importance, let me review yet again my viewpoint on correct and hence enjoyable Stock Exchange participation. The fundamental onus to be discharged by a prospective investor is to select a share whose price has an extremely high probability of showing an increase of at least 40% in one year's time. This is, in point of fact, an extremely severe onus.

Obviously, the share in question must possess some special characteristics for its price to be capable of rising this amount within one year of purchase. The aim of my remaining seven laws is to specify these special characteristics. A share fulfilling the seven laws is to be regarded as one whose financial pedigree is adequate to discharge the onus placed on it. The requirements of these laws are sufficiently stringent to make me feel more than confident of the share's ability to increase its price suitably one year hence.

Thus the crux of successful and hence enjoyable Stock Exchange investment is to select shares of suitable financial pedigree. This selection is made easier if my remaining seven laws are applied. We now proceed with an actual case study.

3.6 Case study no 1: AUTOQUIP

The interim results for the company AUTOQUIP for the six months ended 31 December 1988 appeared in the financial press on 13 March 1989 and are shown in fig 3.1.

We have satisfied Law 2, since we waited for the publication of the most recent set of financial results before considering the share for purchase.

We are now in a position to proceed with Law 3, which concerns the first characteristic that a share of suitable financial pedigree should possess. The most recent results should reflect an increased earnings-per-share and dividend compared with the previous period. My third law can be enunciated as follows:

> ***Law 3:*** *Purchase only those shares which, in their interim or preliminary results, indicate the payment of an increased dividend and have accomplished an increased earnings-per-share.*

We turn now to fig 3.1. For the six months ended 31 December 1988, the earnings-per-share are 7,6 cents. This must be compared with the figure of 4,2 cents for the comparable previous period. *The increase is a magnificent 81%.*

As magnificent an achievement as this 81% increase in earnings-per-share may be, closer examination reveals an even more impressive performance on the part of AUTOQUIP. We see that the number of

Figure 3.1 AUTOQUIP'S interim report and declaration of dividend for the six month period ended 31 December 1988

AUTOQUIP GROUP · LIMITED

(Incorporated in the Republic of South Africa)
(Registration No 87/02838/06)

Interim Report and Declaration of Dividend for the six month period ended 31 December 1988

Group Earnings up 102%

Financial Results

The consolidated unaudited results are as follows:

Consolidated Income Statement

Year ended June 1988 R000's		Half-year ended December 1988 R000's	Half-year ended December 1987 R000's	Percentage Change
22 163	Turnover	**16 413**	10 110	+ 62%
2 588	Operating income	**2 200**	1 234	+ 78%
175	Finance charges	**161**	43	
2 413	Net income before taxation	**2 039**	1 191	+ 71%
904	Taxation	**843**	589	
1 509	Net income after taxation	**1 196**	602	+ 99%
–	Share of income – foreign operations	**20**	–	
1 509	Net income attributable to shareholders	**1 216**	602	+ 102%
480	Dividend	**400**	–	
1 029	Retained income	**816**	602	
14 400	Weighted average number of shares in issue (000's)	**16 000**	14 400	
10,5	Earnings per share (cents)	**7,6**	4,2	+ 81%
3,0	Dividend per share (cents)	**2,5**	–	

Consolidated Balance sheet

June 1988 R000's		December 1988 R000's	December 1987 R000's
	Capital employed		
4 857	Stated capital	**4 857**	4 886
1 029	Distributable reserve	**1 845**	602
5 886	Shareholders' funds	**6 702**	5 488
146	Medium term liabilities	**211**	133
6 032		**6 913**	5 621
	Employment of capital		
1 200	Fixed assets and investments	**1 146**	491
4 832	Net current assets	**5 767**	5 130
12 177	Current assets	**16 496**	10 393
7 345	Current liabilities	**10 729**	5 263
7 345	Interest free	**9 695**	5 263
–	Interest bearing	**1 034**	–
6 032		**6 913**	5 621
36,8	Net tangible asset value per share (cents)	**41,9**	38,3

COMMENTS:

Profile:
The Autoquip division wholesales and retails automotive tyres and accessories. Partquip is a specialist wholesaler of automotive parts, whilst Techniquip is a distributor of industrial bearings and allied products.

Results:
Aggressive niche marketing in all divisions, together with improved stock availibility in the Partquip division have combined to enable the group to achieve excellent results in the six month period to end of December 1988. The group is also reaping the benefits of tightened financial controls as well as a significantly improved buying policy.

Foreign operations:
The group's off-shore associate company, which commenced operations in April 1988, has contributed to overall profits, with full account taken of all start-up costs.

Prospects:
The board is confident that earnings in the period to year-end will at least keep pace with those achieved to date. The Autoquip Vaal branch will commence trading in March 1989 and is expected to make a contribution in the period to year-end.

In addition we expect to experience the full benefit of the synergy between Partquip and Techniquip. It is further anticipated that the off-shore operation will make a considerable contribution in the medium term, as well as offering significant advantages to the group in terms of overseas buying power.

Dividends:
An interim dividend of 2,5 cents has been declared, with a 6,5 cents dividend forecast for the full year. The interim dividend will be paid on 14 April 1989 to shareholders registered on 31 March 1989.

BD Coquelle (*Managing Director*)
GR Coombes (*Director*) 13 March 1989

Registered Office:
6th Floor
Saambou National Building
130 Commissioner St
Johannesburg, 2001

Transfer Secretaries:
Fraser Street Registrars (Pty) Limited
Ground Floor
65 President Street
Johannesburg, 2001

Directors: GJ Santana (Chairman), BD Coquelle (Managing Director), CS Seabrooke, GR Coombes.

shares issued increased from 14,4 million to 16 million during the period under analysis. Thus, *despite* an 11% increase in issued shares, the earnings-per-share managed an 81% jump.

An examination of the net income attributable to shareholders may be employed to indicate the true extent of AUTOQUIP's achievement, since this item precedes a consideration of the number of shares in issue. It is seen to have increased from R0,602 million to R1,216 million, a really magnificent increase of 102%. More than this achievement simply cannot be asked or expected of a company.

To indicate the effect of the increased shares in issue, the following calculations of the respective earnings-per-share figures are useful.

We have

$$\text{earnings-per-share} = \frac{\text{after-tax attributable income}}{\text{number of shares in issue}}$$

Therefore, for the six months ended 31 December 1988 we have

$$\text{earnings-per-share} = \frac{\text{R1,216 million}}{\text{16 million}} = \text{R0,076} = \text{7,6 cents}$$

whereas, for the six months ended 31 December 1987 we have

$$\text{earnings-per-share} = \frac{\text{R0,602 million}}{\text{14,4 million}} = \text{R0,042} = \text{4,2 cents}$$

The reader should be constantly aware of the goal he has set himself regarding his selection of shares. The prime goal is an increase in the share price of at least 40% within one year, and possibly the main ingredient in accomplishing this is an increase in earnings-per-share of a suitable magnitude. *An 81% increase is most certainly to be placed in this category.*

However, the prospective investor must not become over-excited at this early stage. There are still four laws to be applied, and all of these must be satisfied simultaneously before a purchase is to be recommended. In the meantime, however, we must admit that our analysis of AUTOQUIP is revealing a very rosy picture.

3.7 Consideration of the maiden interim dividend declaration

Thus far we have dealt with only half of the requirements of Law 3, namely the required increase in the earnings-per-share, and still have the second half to consider, namely the increase in the dividend declared.

In the case of AUTOQUIP we are in for an extremely pleasant finding in this regard. We read that for the six months ended 31 December 1988 an interim dividend of 2,5 cents has been declared, compared with *zero* cents for the previous comparable period. Such an occurrence merits detailed discussion.

What has actually occurred is that AUTOQUIP has declared an interim dividend *for the first time.* This is referred to as its *maiden* interim dividend. The declaration of a maiden dividend is a cause for celebration, since no company will offer this unless its financial situation is extremely sound.

If we go further and investigate the magnitude of this dividend, we see that it is 2,5 cents. Now for some reading between the lines. Since it is a maiden interim dividend, it could have been 0,5 cents or even 1 cent and still have been completely acceptable to its shareholders, who would have been overjoyed with 1,5 cents and ecstatic with the prospect of as high as 2 cents. However, we see that the maiden is the magnificent sum of 2,5 cents. Even more impressive is the recognition that *this figure is only 0,5 cents less than the total dividend of 3 cents* declared for the whole of the previous 12 month trading period. Thus reading between the lines leads to an exciting conclusion.

In summary, then, more could not have been expected first, of the new earnings-per-share figure of 7,6 cents, and second, of the maiden interim dividend of 2,5 cents.

3.8 Progressing to Law 4

Having passed the stringent hurdle of Law 3, we now consider an even more stringent requirement in the form of Law 4. This concerns the difficult topic of the correct valuation of the share price as at the date of appearance of its most recent financial results. This aspect is of such great importance as to warrant detailed discussion.

We have seen that AUTOQUIP has produced a really superb increase in earnings-per-share and dividend figures, but we still have to cross the hurdle that the share price ruling at the moment of publication of these results might be excessive, notwithstanding their excellence. In other words, the share price might be overvalued by its adherents, in which case there is no point whatsoever in purchasing it. Thus my fourth law is as follows:

> ***Law 4:*** *Consider for purchase only that share whose calculated value is more than its market price.*

The next question, obviously, is: 'How do we calculate the acceptable value of a share?' Eight chapters were devoted to this question in *Winning on the JSE* and it is pointless to repeat this material here. I will merely summarise the conclusions reached therein by considering the example of AUTOQUIP.

The first step in the correct valuation of a share is to *look at the balance sheet*. The following possibilities then arise:

Case 1: If the balance sheet reveals the presence of 'investments' only, the share is to be regarded as a financial share and its correct valuation is obtained using the concept *net asset market value*.

Case 2: If the balance sheet reveals the presence of 'fixed assets' to the exclusion of 'investments', the share is to be regarded as an industrial share and its correct valuation is obtained using the concept *average sectoral earnings and dividend yields*.

Case 3: If the balance sheet reveals the presence of both 'investments' and 'fixed assets', the share is to be regarded as a hybrid share and its correct valuation is obtained using *either* of the two methods above.

The first step in the correct valuation of the AUTOQUIP share is to look at its balance sheet. Figure 3.1 indicates the presence of 'fixed assets and investments'. Thus AUTOQUIP is to be regarded as a hybrid company, amenable to correct valuation by either the net asset market value approach or that of average sectoral yields.

We note, however, that there is no information whatsoever about AUTOQUIP's investments in the financial report in fig 3.1. Thus we are not in a position to calculate net asset market values and the only avenue open to us for share valuation is the earnings and dividend yields method.

In order to determine the earnings yield for the most recent 12 month trading period, the concomitant earnings-per-share figure must be calculated. Figure 3.2 is possibly the most convenient method of achieving this end.

Figure 3.2 Calculation of the earnings-per-share for the most recent 12 month trading period

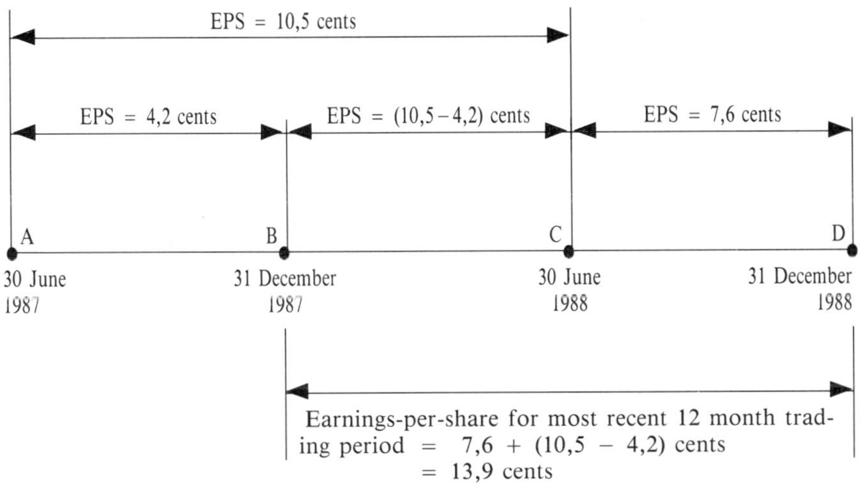

The interpretation of fig 3.2 is as follows: Each six month trading period is annotated in this figure. Thus AB denotes the trading period 30 June 1987 to 31 December 1987, BC the trading period from 31 December 1987 to 30 June 1988, and so on. Thus the most recent 12 month trading period prior to the release of AUTOQUIP's interim results (in fig 3.1) is BD. We know the earnings-per-share for the period CD, since this is given in fig 3.1 as 7,6 cents. However, we do not know the earnings-per-share for the period BC, and *this has to be calculated* as follows.

The results in fig 3.1 indicate that the earnings-per-share for AC are 10,5 cents, and for AB are 4,2 cents. It follows that the required earnings-per-share for the period BC are given by AC – AB, or 10,5 – 4,2 cents, that is 6,3 cents. The required earnings-per-share for the most recent 12 month trading period BD are 6,3 + 7,6, or 13,9 cents.

Now we need to know the price of the AUTOQUIP share on the morning of the appearance of its interim results in fig 3.1. It was 55 cents. Using the earnings-per-share figure of 13,9 cents calculated above, the earnings yield of AUTOQUIP may be calculated as 13,9/55, that is 25,3%.

Having calculated AUTOQUIP's earnings yield for the most recent 12 month trading period, we now need its dividend yield for the same period. Figure 3.1 shows that the total dividend declared for the past 12 months is 3,0+2,5, or 5,5 cents. At its ruling price of 55 cents, this puts AUTOQUIP at a dividend yield of 5,5/55, or 10%.

To summarise, on the day of the appearance of its interim results in fig 3.1, AUTOQUIP stood at an earnings yield of 25,3% and a dividend yield of 10%.

Now we must use these results to determine the acceptable value of the share. Following the detailed discussions in my first book, we must now obtain the average earnings yield and the average dividend yield for the sector in which AUTOQUIP appears on the boards of the Johannesburg Stock Exchange. This sector is denoted 'RETAILERS AND WHOLESALERS'. On the day in question, that is 13 March 1989, the average earnings yield for this sector was given in the financial press as 8,2%, and the average dividend yield as 4,9%.

Comparing its earnings yield of 25,3% with the sector average of a mere 8,2%, and its dividend yield of 10% with the sector average of 4,9%, we see quantitatively that AUTOQUIP is *hopelessly undervalued* by the market at its price of 55 cents.

Thus my stringent Law 4 has been more than satisfied by AUTOQUIP. Things are looking promising indeed, and thus we proceed to a consideration of Law 5.

3.9 Progressing to Law 5

A very strange occurrence is often observed upon publication of a company's financial results. Inevitably there will be a shareholder who, no matter the quantitative degree of excellence of these results, was expecting even better. This disenchanted shareholder proceeds to sell his shares, no matter how unreasonable his expectations of an even better performance may be. Quite unexpectedly, therefore, instead of rising, as the knowledgeable analyst of the company's financial results would anticipate, the share price actually falls, and often by a considerable amount.

This is precisely where I enjoy taking complete advantage of the seller's ignorance of financial analysis, and I will normally take up all the completely unjustified share sales if my finances permit me to do so. This is a fine example of what I discussed in 1.5 of this text; I am quite deliberately acquiring what the seller no longer wants. In even stronger terms, *I want what he is discarding*. I am doing this purely and simply because quantitatively I know exactly what the correct value of the share being sold is, and the seller, because of his ignorance in this matter, has no idea of what it should be. *His loss is my gain* – it is as simple as that. If, at the end of the day, or of the week, my perception of the situation has proved to be correct, as evidenced by the ultimate rise in the share price, my self-image increases to a degree commensurate with the number of his shares I have acquired.

My Law 5 encapsulates the feelings of the above paragraphs. I enunciate it in the following form:

> *Law 5: Realise that the market price of a share can move in an illogical manner. Have the confidence of your calculations to make the most of such a situation, once again realising that logic must and will ultimately return to the market.*

3.10 Now to Law 6

Law 6 relates directly to the financial soundness of the company under consideration. I do not like a company *whose long-term loans are more than 20% of its share capital and reserves*. My readers may ask why I have specified a figure of 20%. My answer is that it has emerged from purely experimental observations over a long period. In this matter I award myself the 'QBE' degree. My readers will most certainly know about that meritorious award termed the OBE – here we are dealing with an award of possibly even more pragmatic excellence, that of being 'Qualified By Experience'! On the basis of my QBE qualification, I would request the prospective Stock Exchange investor to obey this law to the letter!

Thus my sixth law is the following:

> ***Law 6:*** *Do not purchase shares in a company whose long-term loans are more than some 20% of its share capital and reserves.*

To see whether AUTOQUIP fulfils this requirement, we must now look at the balance sheet in fig 3.1. Here we see that the long-term loans are only R0,211 million, while the share capital and reserves are R6,702 million. The ratio is 0,211/6,702, or 3,15%. This is superbly low, and hence Law 6 is more than satisfied by AUTOQUIP.

3.11 Progressing to Law 7

Law 7, too, is a direct reflection of the competence of the company being analysed, this time of its efficiency in utilising the capital available to it. I enunciate this law in the following form:

> ***Law 7:*** *Do not purchase shares in a company whose pre-tax return on capital employed is less than 15%.*

In defence of this quantitative statement of this law, once again I turn to my QBE award.

In the case of AUTOQUIP, fig 3.1 offers the following information in this regard. We have to use the same procedure indicated in fig 3.2 for ascertaining the earnings-per-share figure for the most recent 12 month trading period to determine the pre-tax profits for this same period.

Using the procedure in fig 3.2, we see that the pre-tax profit for the most recent 12 month trading period emerges as R2,039 + (R2,413 – R1,191) million, that is as R3,261 million. Since the total capital employed to achieve these profits was R6,913 million, the pre-tax return on capital employed, in terms of Law 7 above, emerges as 3,261/6,913, that is 47%. *This represents a magnificent achievement.*

Once again AUTOQUIP has more than satisfied a law.

3.12 Now to Law 8

My eighth law pertains to the tradeability of the share in question. It is obviously desirable to possess only that type of share which enjoys some degree of interest among those participating in the Stock Exchange. This law is as follows:

> *Law 8: Do not purchase a share whose weekly traded volume is less than some 20 000.*

Reference to the relevant financial newspapers shows that AUTOQUIP fulfils this requirement.

3.13 My ninth and last law

The ninth law must be fulfilled just prior to an investor's purchase of a share which has satisfied the stringent requirements of the first eight laws. This last law concerns an *overview* of the company itself, its *modus operandi*, its field of operations, its future prospects and any other consideration which the prospective purchaser of shares in it would like to investigate for himself. No two participants will have the same items of analysis on their lists. A very fussy investor will even investigate the merits of the members of the board of directors involved; others will be satisfied with a less intensive research project.

I am an engineer by formal professional training. As a result, I am more inclined towards companies involved in the manufacture, repair or sale of items relevant to the engineering industry. AUTOQUIP falls into the automotive sphere of this industry, and what more exciting avenue can there be when the tendency among car owners is towards do it yourself action in the light of extremely high new car prices?

Thus Law 9 is as follows:

> *Law 9: Have some knowledge of the company concerned. Satisfy yourself about its history, track record and actual modus operandi.*

The reader can ascertain for himself the answers he is seeking to satisfy my Law 9 by analysing the comments offered by the directors in the remaining portion of the report in fig 3.1. These comments more than satisfied my own scrutiny.

3.14 The upshot regarding AUTOQUIP

My reader must want to know what happened regarding my purchases of AUTOQUIP. I purchased what I regarded as a requisite amount at 55 cents and 60 cents on 13 and 14 March 1989. At the week's close the share had increased to 70 cents, a remarkable rise of 27% on the initial purchase price. But more on this score in the following chapters.

3.15 Do not use the concept 'net tangible asset value per share'

There is only one concept in the financial statements in fig 3.1 that we have not used, and this omission is completely deliberate. I refer to the concept 'net tangible asset value per share'. Let me tell you why.

Consider, initially, the income statement for the year ended June 1988. We see that 'retained income' at the year end is given as R1,029 million. Where does this amount go? It goes into what are esoterically termed the 'distributable reserves'. Now look at the balance sheet. Under the section 'Capital employed', we have the following:

Capital employed	**R million**
Stated capital	4,857
Distributable reserves	1,029
Shareholders' funds	5,886

Thus the *total shareholders' funds* as at the end of the June 1988 financial year were R5,886 million. This is precisely the manner in which I would record this state of affairs.

But now convention steps in to bring about the following difficult situation. First, these total shareholders' funds are to be divided by the total number of issued shares. I have no difficulty with this, provided that the outcome is to be termed 'total shareholders' funds per share', since this is precisely what this operation entails. Thus this quantity of total shareholders' funds per share for AUTOQUIP as at 30 June 1988 would be the amount of R5,886 million derived above divided by the total number of issued shares, which we are informed in fig 3.1 is 14,4 million as of that date. The outcome is R5,886/14,4, that is R0,409 or 40,9 cents.

I see no use whatsoever in this figure, but provided it is accurately termed 'total shareholders' funds per share' I take no mathematical umbrage at all. I do take such umbrage, however, when the outcome of this arithmetical operation is labelled by some other name. Figure 3.1 indicates that the directors of AUTOQUIP use the label 'net tangible asset value per share'. I must disagree with this in no uncertain terms. There is nothing tangible in this figure at all.

But now this state of affairs is compounded even further by some companies calling this total shareholders' funds per share figure the 'net worth per share'. The effect on an ignorant Stock Exchange participant can only be imagined. He would obviously be of the opinion that the above calculated figure of 40,9 cents represents what would conventionally be interpreted as 'net worth per share'.

In all my twenty years of share analysis I have never found occasion to use the concept 'total shareholders' funds per share', let alone its mislabelling as either 'net tangible asset value per share' or even worse 'net worth per share'. Therefore I would ask my readers to ignore this completely. It is simultaneously irrelevant and misleading. A more adverse comment cannot be made.

In passing, it is to be pointed out that the directors have miscalculated the total shareholders' funds per share in fig 3.1 for the period ended 30 June 1988. The figure of 36,8 cents appearing therein can be shown to arise out of the incorrect use of the figure 16 million for the number of issued shares, as opposed to the correct number of 14,4 million, as stated.

We return now to a further consideration of fig 3.1. We see that six months later the amount to be retained by the company is R0,816 million. The total distributable reserve is now the previous R1,029 million plus this new figure, standing at R1,845 million. The new figure for the total shareholders' funds is then the share capital of R4,857 million, which has obviously remained unchanged, plus the new distributable reserve of R1,845 million, to total R6,702 million as indicated in fig 3.1.

My manner of reporting on this state of affairs would be that the total shareholders' funds of R6,792 million as at 31 December 1988 represented an increase of 13,9% over those of R5,886 million as at 30 June 1988. I certainly would not state that the new net tangible asset value per share was 41,9 cents compared with the previous 40,9 cents.

4

The difficult topic of South African tax analysis

Page

4.1 Introduction

Possibly the best manner to begin this chapter is with the well-known adage: 'He who would want to live in peace must prepare for war.'

This war situation may arise when a Stock Exchange participant decides to sell some of his shares. Inland Revenue has no objection whatsoever to his purchasing these shares; it is only *when he sells them at a profit* that storm clouds may gather on the horizon.

To his horror, the Stock Exchange participant may find himself enmeshed in the following state of affairs. Inland Revenue requests of the taxpayer on his income tax return information regarding all sales of shares by him during the previous financial year. The taxpayer is obligated to disclose all details of such sales, and customarily does so with pleasure.

On receiving his tax assessment some months later, he may be horrified to find that Inland Revenue *has added the profits on his Stock Exchange share sales to his normal taxable income*, and has levied the tax payable on this new, and conventionally greatly increased, figure.

According to South African income tax law, a Stock Exchange participant is obligated, first, to render payment in full of the figure as calculated by Inland Revenue. Only then is he entitled to object to what he obviously regards as the horrendous and unjustified procedure of having the realised profits on his share sales regarded as additional taxable income. He must then proceed to the Special Tax Court, at his own expense (which may often be considerable), to prove why these profits should be free of tax.

Again I point out the tremendous stringency of the situation faced by all South African taxpayers; *they are at all times guilty until proved innocent*. The onus always rests on the taxpayer's shoulders to prove that Inland Revenue is wrong, and this to compound matters further, only after he has rendered payment in full for what he regards as Inland Revenue's incorrect assessment of his taxable income.

It is in order to avoid such a devastating state of affairs with regard to Stock Exchange investments that fundamental income tax considerations are discussed in detail in this chapter.

4.2 Capital assets and revenue assets

In contrast to most other writers, I consider the most fundamental starting point of an analysis of South African income tax law to be the definition of a *capital* asset, on the one hand, as opposed to that of a *revenue* asset, on the other.

This matter is of such fundamental importance, and often difficulty, that the South African Tax Act does not even attempt to define these two diametrically opposite categories. It is left to case law to propose a logical and all-embracing structure upon which to base future argument.

All the assets possessed by a taxpayer fall into one of only two categories, namely 'capital' and 'revenue'. Since there is no third category, any difficulty which may arise in the attempted classification of an asset can often be resolved by the adoption of the '*reductio ad absurdem*' approach. That is, if, for example, I am experiencing difficulty with the capital asset definition in a given instance, I try the revenue asset approach. If this latter works, then by exclusion my problem has been solved. But more on this score, in great detail, in what follows.

4.3 The definition pertains to the asset's owner and not to the asset itself

At first sight this concept may prove difficult for many readers. Therefore I start with some extremely simple and easily recognised situations.

Take a person who collects stamps as a hobby. He purchases a set of stamps to supplement his existing collection. Now for the first and most fundamental question, which more often than not proves exceptionally difficult to answer: *Why has this person purchased his new asset?* In case some readers are perplexed at what may seem to be a most ridiculous question, let me indicate that it is often at this very first step that most asset tax problems with Inland Revenue can be resolved.

The stamp collector may stand aghast at my question. Quite obviously, he cries vehemently, he bought the stamps to augment his collection. In turn, he did this because he was attracted to them.

Now my next fundamental question: *Was there any thought of selling them at some future occasion?* The use of the word 'selling' here tacitly means 'at a profit'.

The stamp collector may stand aghast at the thought of selling his newly acquired and beloved stamps, of which he is extremely proud, at a profit. Most definitely not! he exclaims.

On the basis of this explanation, Inland Revenue would be quite content to classify these stamps *in the hands of our hobbyist* as a capital asset. This latter vital codicil must be noted and appreciated.

We are in a position, now, to state the prime requirement of the definition of a capital asset:

> *A capital asset is one which has been acquired not for purpose of resale at a profit.*

Thus it is the *intention of its new owner* that has decided the classification of the asset under consideration.

4.4 The definition of a revenue asset

Since the definition of a revenue asset is diametrically opposite to that of a capital asset, we have merely to exclude the word 'not' appearing in the above definition of the latter to obtain that of a revenue asset:

> *A revenue asset is one which has been acquired for purpose of resale at a profit.*

As an obvious example of a revenue asset, let us now consider the example of the same stamps of the previous situation being purchased by a stamp *dealer*. His only motive for this purchase is to sell the stamps at a later date *at a profit*. This latter type of sale provides him with his livelihood, since, after all, he is a stamp dealer.

Thus one and the same asset is classified as a *capital* asset in the hands of the hobbyist, but as a *revenue* asset in the hands of the stamp dealer. It was the diametrically opposite intention of each of these persons when purchasing the same stamps that resulted in the diametrically opposite classification of the asset in each case.

In tax circles, the esoteric name for a revenue asset is 'stock in trade'. Its meaning is obvious. A revenue asset is one which a dealer who trades in that asset would use as his stock.

4.5 But is it really all that clear-cut?

Now we will introduce some possible complications into our hobbyist example. Let us assume that our proud stamp collector shows off his albums some months later. One viewer is so impressed with the hobbyist's additions that he offers him an extremely high price for the latter in an attempt to procure the sale. Our hobbyist, previously so proud of the new additions to his collection, yields, primarily because of the high offer, and parts with the aforesaid stamps at a great profit. *What happens to the capital asset classification of these stamps?*

We are in a position to answer this question from two different points of view. First, at the time of his acquisition of the stamps our hobbyist can honestly state that there was no intention to resell them at a profit. But please anticipate now the equally acceptable and honest reply of Inland Revenue in this regard. While the *first* time round did possibly and in all feasibility not contain the element of resale at a profit, any *future purchase* of stamps must now surely contain the element of such possible resale. In other words, Inland Revenue will be watching our stamp hobbyist's future actions extremely closely. To put this matter another way, it is the *frequency of such sales* that will either exonerate or condemn him. We must appreciate the difficulty facing Inland Revenue in such matters. *Often the stated intention of the purchaser of an asset does not match up with his acts in the future.*

The second method of answering the question is to see whether the definition of a revenue asset matches the situation pertaining. On this first occasion I feel the hobbyist can escape the accusation that these stamps were purchased to be his stock in trade. Seeing that he was not a recognised dealer at that moment, the revenue asset classification does not hold, and hence by exclusion the capital asset classification does.

But the next time our hobbyist sells his stamps at a profit may well seal his fate.

4.6 Why the insistence on a clear-cut classification of an asset?

My readers may well be asking: 'Why are you so intent on getting an absolutely clear and definitive classification of an asset?' The answer stems from the following crucial principle in tax law:

> *Accruals resulting from the sale at a profit of a capital asset are classified as capital accruals, and hence escape tax. Accruals resulting from the sale of a revenue asset are accruals of a revenue nature, that is income, and hence taxable.*

The vital reason for establishing at the outset the clear-cut definition of a newly acquired asset then becomes obvious to its owner.

To facilitate further the manner of arriving at the required classification of the asset, I now combine and amplify further the two questions asked of the new owner in 4.3:

> *Was the asset in question acquired with the prime intention of resale at a profit on some future occasion? If not, what was the purpose of the acquisition?*

This is precisely the question that Inland Revenue will be putting to those taxpayers who consistently claim that their sales of assets represented accruals of a capital nature, since these assets were capital assets. The taxpayer must be doubly sure of his standpoint here, since the onus is on him to prove this once Inland Revenue states in his most recent tax assessment that it is of the opposite opinion.

4.7 Some typical examples of capital assets

In the light of the importance of this topic, let us review some typical purchases made by a taxpayer.

First, his house. If this was purchased in the first instance to be home to himself and his family, his onus has been discharged quite definitively, and the house becomes a capital asset. Obviously, as his family grows the house may become too small, and hence a sale at some time in the future is more than possible. Inland Revenue will permit this, since at the time of that he first acquired it, the taxpayer's honest intention was to use this house as a home, with all the connotations hereof. Any profits which arise upon this future sale will quite definitely be regarded as accruals of a capital nature and hence escape tax.

But note the codicil. This benevolence on the part of Inland Revenue will most certainly not apply if our taxpayer buys and sells his so-called 'home' regularly, of the order, for example, of every three years or so. The taxpayer must thus be called upon to realise the fatuous nature of his 'capital asset' claims under such circumstances. Once he is made to understand that an outlook of honesty must prevail for him to succeed in his attempts to discharge the extremely severe onus which South African tax law places on him, I am certain that the type of taxpayer whose purchases and resales of his house are of such frequency that his actions can only be called 'sailing extremely close to the wind', will desist therefrom in view of the severe penalties involved.

As a second example we consider the taxpayer's car. Once again, upon acquiring the car he quite obviously realises that at some time in the future he will sell it and acquire a replacement. This latter sale may even be at a profit compared with its purchase price. However, since his intention was completely acceptable at the time of acquisition, namely to obtain a very necessary means of transport, his car is a capital asset. Once again, the frequency of sale and subsequent repurchase may negate this capital asset classification.

Finally, we come to a consideration of the taxpayer's shares on the Stock Exchange. Will these be regarded as assets of a capital, or of the diametrically opposed revenue, classification? The topic is of such depth and importance that the following sections are devoted to its consideration.

4.8 Inland Revenue and the private taxpayer's Stock Exchange operations

In commencing the intricacies of Inland Revenue versus the private taxpayer, which can be lengthy, subtle and often apparently illogical at first sight if the necessary precautions are not taken *ab initio*, I must point out my prime requirement in this regard. This is that all Stock Exchange participation by our private taxpayer shall be what I have termed 'correct' participation. That is, *all the shares that he purchases should obey all the nine laws which I enunciate in considerable detail in chapter 3.*

This requirement represents the cardinal point of all my future argument concerning Inland Revenue and the attitude it adopts towards the private Stock Exchange participant. *If it is not fulfilled, all of what follows automatically becomes null and void.* I cannot stress this vital aspect adequately.

Therefore I base my detailed exposition on this involved subject on the fundamental assumption that my nine laws have been implicitly obeyed by the reader in his incursions into the Stock Exchange.

I commence with the concrete example of my purchases of AUTOQUIP shares at 55 and 60 cents on 13 and 14 March 1989, as indicated in 3.14. As with all such share purchases, the fundamental onus I now have to discharge is to answer the vital question posed in 4.6, where the crucial property of a capital asset is first broached in this text. This is, then: *Was the asset in question acquired with the prime intention of resale at a profit on some future occasion. If not, what was the purpose of the acquisition?*

Obviously I must offer an accurate and honest answer to this question. The definition here of an 'accurate and honest answer' is one that will stand up to the most intense and hectic scrutiny and cross-examination by the most ardent member of the legal profession in the most severe situation of my appearance in the Special Tax Court. I certainly do not envisage such an event taking place; in fact, I ardently trust it will never come to such a state of affairs. But note that it is in order to prevent such a nerve-wracking and horrendous occurrence that correctly operating Stock Exchange participants, among which I am to be counted, must take the precautions below.

My honest and accurate answer to the important question posed above is the following: No, I most definitely did not acquire the AUTOQUIP shares with the *prime* intention of resale at a profit on some future occasion. Right, says Inland Revenue, then please offer us your explanation of the purpose of your acquisition of these shares.

Now I refer Inland Revenue to the contents of 3.2. In the presence of my own family's inflation rate of 31%, I have resorted to the purchase of the above-mentioned AUTOQUIP shares *in order to obtain a real return on my finances*. Now a crucial observation and statement:

> *For as long as AUTOQUIP is capable of accomplishing this real return for me, I most definitely have no intention of selling them in the future.*

But please note the codicil in my answer. If at some stage in the future (and obviously I hope and trust that such a stage will never be reached), for some reason which remains hidden at the present, some detrimental financial transactions are to prevent AUTOQUIP from accomplishing what I require, I request the right to sell the shares without incurring the wrath of Inland Revenue.

Thus I am being completely honest with Inland Revenue. It is far simpler for me to sit back, now that I have selected my AUTOQUIP shares following the detailed and lengthy selection procedure indicated in chapter 3, and merely watch the progress I require and expect of these shares. I most certainly do not want to go through the same procedure again soon if I can help it. In addition, I most certainly do not wish to incur the approximate 4% charges which will be involved in my selling these shares and purchasing suitable replacements.

To summarise my answer, I have selected my AUTOQUIP shares on what can only be termed a detailed and scientific basis. For this reason I am of the firm belief that there is an extremely high probability of AUTOQUIP discharging the onus I have placed on it. However, should the unexpected occur, and for some presently unanticipated reason this latter onus at some stage not be adequately discharged, I request the right to sell these shares and replace them, if possible, with an alternative which does satisfy the requirements of my nine laws.

4.9 The vital role of the dividend income return

I now proceed even further to convince Inland Revenue of the sincerity and honesty of the answer I gave in the previous section. This relates to the *magnitude of the dividend return* which I am to receive from my involvement with the AUTOQUIP shares.

I have parted with a considerable sum of my finances in order to acquire these shares. In esoteric circles this is referred to as my *capital involvement* in this financial transaction. I use the word 'involvement' quite deliberately here instead of another which the reader might have been anticipating. The specification of this latter word will be made now.

Am I prepared to allow my capital sum to lie fallow while my prime requirement of a suitable real return on it occurs?

We have just reached an important point in the argument. It must be realised that my aim of a real return on my finances can be achieved *purely and simply by the rise in price of the AUTOQUIP share.* In esoteric phraseology, this state of affairs would be described as a real return being provided by the capital appreciation alone.

I now use the word 'investor' for the first time in this discussion. A really competent investor would require of his capital that it is not allowed to lie fallow, but instead should *provide him with an annual income in addition to the aforesaid capital appreciation.* There is an old but extremely valid saying: capital appreciation cannot provide its owner with his meals in the interim period; income derived therefrom can.

In order to be counted among these competent investors, I thus require of my finances tied up in the purchase of the AUTOQUIP shares that, in addition to the capital appreciation expected via an increase in the share price, they afford me *an annual income by suitable dividend declarations.*

My Law 4, concerning the correct valuation of the share price in question, has ensured that my dividend return in this regard *is better than that provided by the average dividend yield* of the section of the Stock Exchange under which the share is listed. Thus 3.8 calculated that at the time of purchase my dividend return on AUTOQUIP would be 10%, compared with the figure of 4,9% for the average dividend yield of the RETAILERS AND WHOLESALERS sector in which this share is housed.

Strange as it may seem, and despite its great importance in taxation and other related financial matters, there is no real *de jure* definition of an 'investor'. There is, however, what may be called a *de facto* definition, and one of which Inland Revenue is apparently extremely proud. This is that an investor is *that person who receives an annual income on his capital involvements.* The degree of competency of this investor shall then be judged by the *percentage return* which this annual income affords him.

We have just landed, as far as Inland Revenue is concerned, in a most contentious financial minefield. This topic is so intricate that it will be discussed in more detail later in the text, but for the moment it is highly appropriate to indicate its presence at this juncture. It concerns an asset which its owner purports to be a capital asset, but from which *no annual income is derived.* To judge from the most recent case law studies, Inland Revenue would appear to be most unhappy in awarding this type of person that most valuable and sought-after definition of 'investor'.

A typical example of such a situation is the purchase of Kruger rands. A review of the relevant case law will indicate that virtually the only manner by which the owner can discharge the onus required of him by Inland Revenue is the *length of time* for which he held his Kruger rands prior to selling them. This restriction of time is often found to be so stringent that the proceeds of the sale are invariably regarded as accruals of a revenue nature, and hence taxable, as opposed to the owner's assertion of accruals of a capital nature. This issue will be taken up in considerable detail later, when the purchase of what are termed 'blue chip' shares, with their very low dividend yields, is analysed.

For the moment, however, I return to the consideration of the purchase of my AUTOQUIP shares, which is the concrete example under discussion here. The fact that I am to receive an annual income by way of dividends which is more than double the average dividend yield of that sector in which these shares are listed, confers upon me, even according to the stringent standards of Inland Revenue, the label 'competent investor'. This greatly aids my reply to that all-important question posed by Inland Revenue: 'Was the asset in question acquired with the prime intention of resale at a profit on some future occasion? If not, what was the purpose of the acquisition?'

I am now in the extremely favourable position to reply as follows: The asset in question was *not* purchased with the prime intention of resale at a profit on some future occasion. It was purchased, *first*, with the prime motive of providing me with a real return on my finances involved via its expected capital appreciation due to the anticipated increase in share price, and *second*, to provide me with an annual income in the form of a greater-than-average dividend yield. This latter consideration bestows on me that highly desirable label 'investor' by Inland Revenue, and it is this status which causes Inland Revenue to view any future actions by me with regard to my AUTOQUIP shares in a favourable light. All in all, then, I stand convinced that I have discharged the onus required of me to have my purchase of AUTOQUIP shares classified as *the acquisition of a capital asset.*

Such a definition is awarded *at the moment of purchase* of my AUTOQUIP shares. It is not a *post hoc* definition. This aspect is of such importance that it warrants further discussion. Some readers may be of the opinion that I must wait some time for Inland Revenue to class my AUTOQUIP share purchase as the acquisition of a capital asset, possibly on the basis of my future actions. This is not so. Provided I can satisfy Inland Revenue regarding the oft-repeated important question enunciated earlier, the *desired label of a capital asset is of application from the moment of my share purchase.*

I end this chapter with the important observation that there is another advantage to be gained from the application of my nine laws of share purchase. This is that, provided the owner is not of the prime intention to resell them at a profit, the shares so purchased *automatically* receive the desired classification 'capital asset'.

5

Further intricacies of South African tax law for the Stock Exchange investor: the sale of a capital asset

5.1 Introduction

This chapter deals with the situation faced by many knowledgeable Stock Exchange investors between July and September 1987.

At this time share prices were rising at a rate which the knowledgeable realised was too steep to be either justifiable or maintainable. Obviously a crash was in the offing, and hence they wished to sell their shares. This course of action would enable them first, to avail themselves of the extremely high prices pertaining, and second, to avoid the precipitous fall in prices which just had to occur. In other words the knowledgeable realised that the rampant bull market of July 1987 was at its peak, and that the normal disastrous consequences would follow.

Now the all-important question: Would Inland Revenue declare their realised profits on these share sales to be accruals of a revenue nature, and hence subject to tax? The difficulty of the answer to this question was compounded by the fact that many Stock Exchange participants had only entered the market in approximately January 1987 on seeing that the various sectoral indices were beginning an extremely promising climb. An additional complicating feature was that because of this promising climb, large sums of money were involved.

It appeared that Inland Revenue could either react in a lenient manner, or take a strict and severe stance. The issue revolved around the crucial question: Would the sale of previously defined capital assets be permitted?

This chapter attempts to answer the above two questions. Extracts from judgments of the Appellate Division which are deemed relevant will be quoted to provide a sound and logical basis for the discussion.

5.2 The change of intention that has occurred

Chapter 4 indicated that a capital asset definition occurs when the prime intention underlying the acquisition of an asset was not resale at a profit.

The owner of a share purchased on this basis in December 1986, and hence regarded as a capital asset, suddenly wishes to sell this share in July 1987. *Obviously a change of intention has occurred.* Is such a change of intention permissible without incurring the wrath of Inland Revenue?

The 1976 case[1] of *John Bell and Co v Secretary of Inland Revenue* provides the first answer I am to use here. In his judgment at page 429, *Wessels*, JA states:

> Moreover, my understanding of the cases that deal with the matter is that the mere change of intention to dispose of an asset hitherto held as capital does not *per se* subject the resultant profit to tax. Something more is required in order to metamorphose the character of the asset and so render its proceeds gross income. For example, the taxpayer must already be trading in the same or similar kinds of assets, or he then and there starts some trade or business or embarks on some scheme for selling such assets for profit, and, in either case, the asset in question is taken into or used as his stock-in-trade.

In 1978 in the case[2] of *Elandsheuwel Farming v Secretary of Inland Revenue*, *Trollip*, JA refers to the above judgment and states at pages 114 and 115:

> Of course, every decision by an owner to dispose of an asset held as a capital asset does involve a change of intention; hitherto his intention has been to retain it as such; now he changes that intention by deciding to dispose of it. According to the above-mentioned *dicta* a mere change of intention of that kind does not *per se* subject any resultant gain to tax; something more is required for that to happen. That additional factor is usually something indicating that the disposal is in reality in pursuance of some trade or business or scheme for making profit. The intervention of such an additional factor may be indicated by the circumstances surrounding the change of intention or in the way in which it was manifested or carried out.

Therefore it becomes apparent that a shareholder who previously held his shares as a capital asset because of his initial intention of holding them and not reselling them at a profit, *is permitted to change this intention* and to sell his shares.

5.3 The dictum 'to the best advantage'

The judgments quoted in 5.2 provide the first item in the armamentarium of the correctly operating shareholder who wishes to sell his shares. We now come to the second item. Case law actually provides the shareholder with an acceptable reason for his change of intention, giving him the second item in his armamentarium. This is what I describe as the dictum '*to the best advantage*', and it arises as explained below.

Conventionally, a shareholder will not decide out of the blue to sell shares previously held as a capital asset. A set of circumstances must have arisen which, when appraised logically, convinced him that it would be in his best interests to sell his shares. Such appraisal would inevitably be of the form described in the judgments below.

Possibly the earliest judgment expressing permission to the shareholder to sell his shares is that given by *Wessels*, JA in the case[3] of *Commissioner of Inland Revenue v Stott* in 1928:

> Every person who invests his surplus funds in land or stock or any other asset is entitled to realise such asset to the best advantage and to accommodate the asset to the exigencies of the market in which he is selling. The fact that he does so cannot alter what is an investment of capital into a trade or business for earning profits.

The phrase '*to the best advantage*' is all-important. The shareholders mentioned in 5.1 who were sufficiently knowledgeable to realise in July 1987 that an unstable and rampant bull market existed on the Johannesburg Stock Exchange and hence wished to sell their previously defined capital asset shares in order to realise maximum profits, quite incontrovertibly fall into the category of being entitled '*to realise such asset to the best advantage and to accommodate the asset to the exigencies of the market in which he is selling*'. In my mind there is no question whatsoever but that this quoted judgment applies to the shareholders whose predicament with regard to the 1987 Johannesburg Stock Exchange bull market was detailed above.

I consider this second item in the armamentarium of the correctly operating Stock Exchange investor an extremely potent one. Thus I am surprised that it has not been applied more frequently than a review of the relevant law case studies reveals.

In 1975, *Holmes*, JA confirms the above dictum of *Wessels*, JA, and in the case[4] of *Natal Estates Ltd v Secretary of Inland Revenue* states the following:

> It is undoubtedly correct that if, on the facts of a given case, the most that can be said is that the taxpayer was merely realising a capital asset to the best advantage, the proceeds do not become part of his gross income.

In 1976, in the case[1] of *John Bell and Co v Secretary of Inland Revenue*, we have the following judgment of *Wessels*, JA:

> The mere fact, therefore, that a person deliberately delays the disposal of a capital asset because, upon his reading of the property market, the 'hand of time' is needed in order to realise the asset to best advantage cannot, in my opinion, result in a change in the character of the asset so as to alter it from a capital asset, held for the purpose of advantageous disposal, to stock-in-trade, held for the purpose of earning income in the course of an operation of business in carrying out a scheme for profit-making.

In order to assist the reader in realising his strengths should his sales of shares purchased according to my nine laws ever be questioned by Inland Revenue, the following section summarises the argument of the text thus far.

5.4 Strengths in the correctly operating shareholder's armamentarium

The correctly operating shareholder will have purchased his shares according to my nine laws. Seeing that his prime intention was not to resell these shares at a profit, *from the very outset* they will have been defined accurately and correctly as capital assets.

At some later stage events may occur which were not anticipated at the time of the above share purchases. These events could lead our shareholder to the conclusion that by selling all or some of his shares now, he could realise these capital assets to best advantage. He is permitted, in terms of the above-quoted judgments, to *change his initial intention without invalidating the original classification of 'capital asset' of his shares.*

Thus, despite this stated change of intention, the profits he will realise on the sale of his shares will still be regarded as accruals of a capital nature, and hence will not be taxable in his hands.

The prime stipulation he will have to obey is that *he is not taking part in a scheme of profit-making.* This latter stipulation is of such importance that it is the topic of the following section.

5.5 Tax implications of the sale of shares previously held as capital assets

Possibly the most comprehensive judgment in this matter is that of *Corbett*, JA, once again in the case[2] of *Elandsheuwel Farming v Secretary of Inland Revenue.* At page 118 we read the following:

> Where a taxpayer sells property, the question as to whether the profits derived from the sale are taxable in his hands by reason of the proceeds constituting gross income, or are not subject to tax because the proceeds constitute receipts or accruals of a capital nature, turns on the further enquiry as to whether the sale amounted to the realisation of a capital asset or whether it was the sale of an asset in the course of carrying on a business or in pursuance of a profit-making scheme. Where a single transaction is involved it is usually more appropriate to limit the enquiry to the simple alternatives of a capital realisation or a profit-making scheme. In its normal and most straightforward form, the latter connotes the acquisition of an asset for the purpose of reselling it at a profit. This profit is then the result of the productive turnover of the capital represented by the asset, and consequently falls into the category of income. The asset constitutes in effect the taxpayer's stock-in-trade or floating capital. In contrast to this the sale of an asset, acquired with a view to holding it either in a non-productive state or in order to derive income from the productive use thereof, and in fact so held, constitutes a realisation of fixed capital and the proceeds an accrual of a capital nature.

> In the determination of the question into which of these two classes a particular transaction falls, the intention of the taxpayer, both at the time of acquiring the asset and at the time of its sale, is of great, and sometimes decisive, importance. Other significant factors include, *inter alia*, the actual activities of the taxpayer in relation to the asset in question, the manner of its realisation, the taxpayer's other business operations (if any) and, in the case of a company, its objects as laid down in its memorandum of association. The aforegoing principles are trite and require no supportive citation of authority. They have been stated and restated, in various forms, by the Court on numerous occasions.

The shareholder must ensure, therefore, that the sale of his shares 'amounted to the realisation of a capital asset' and that it was most definitely not 'the sale of an asset in the course of carrying on a business or in pursuance of a profit-making scheme'.

Please note, however, that it is not only to his own satisfaction that the shareholder must discharge this '*not in a scheme of profit-making*' onus, but to the far more searching and demanding satisfaction of Inland Revenue. Hence the contents of the second paragraph of the judgment quoted above come to be of paramount importance. I cannot stress adequately the hold that Inland Revenue has in this connection over the slightly off-course shareholder. Should Inland Revenue be even slightly perturbed about the mere hint of a possibility of the existence of 'a scheme of profit-making', very soon that shareholder will find himself in the horrendous position of being guilty until proved innocent.

For this reason I insist that in order to enjoy his operations on the Stock Exchange, an investor must not only obey all my nine laws, but also act in the honest manner expected of him by Inland Revenue. Only then will the spirit of enjoyment prevail, as will non-interference by Inland Revenue in his 40% per annum accruals from his share operations.

5.6 A judgment referring specifically to share transactions

The judgments quoted above do not refer specifically to share transactions on the Stock Exchange, although this situation is covered in the general discussion. A judgment dealing specifically with such share transactions, and which, in my opinion, is an important one for its clear dissection of the aspects to be covered, is that given by *Friedman*, J in June 1983 in the Natal Special Court for Income Tax Appeals. It is *ITC* 1412, and the judgment contains the following important elements:

> The most important test employed by the courts in deciding whether or not the proceeds arising from the disposal of an asset are income or capital is the test of intention with which the asset was acquired. While this intention may not always be conclusive, generally speaking it is the decisive factor. The fact that, in order to establish an asset to be of a capital nature, the taxpayer must show that he acquired it with the intention to hold it, does not mean that at the time the taxpayer acquired the asset he must have excluded any thought of possibly selling it in future at a profit. Very often (indeed it is perhaps usual even where a taxpayer acquires a capital asset), he forsees the possibility that with the ravages of inflation and the erosion of money, that asset will grow in value in the sense that its monetary value will increase and that he may one day, therefore, be able to sell it at a price greater than the price at which he acquired it. The fact that the taxpayer, in acquiring the asset foresees these possibilities, will not in itself render the asset thereby something other than capital.

Of vital importance are the sentences: 'Very often . . . he foresees the possibility that that asset will grow in value . . . and that he may one day be able to sell it at a price greater than the price at which he acquired it. The fact that the taxpayer, in acquiring the asset foresees these possibilities, will not in itself render the asset thereby something other than capital.' In my opinion the above dictum is crucial to the correctly operating shareholder, and henceforth I term it the '*foreseeing the possibility*' dictum.

The judgment now continues with a discussion of the cardinal onus to be discharged by the taxpayer:

> The burden of proving the intention with which an asset was acquired, and of its nature, is upon the taxpayer, and this burden must be discharged by him on a balance of probability. The taxpayer's own evidence as to his intention is of course important, but it is by no means decisive. Very often the taxpayer may have no clear idea as to his intention. His recollection may be uncertain and it may be faulty, and more often than not what he says in the witness box to have been his intention is more the product of reconstruction than of positive recollection. The Court must therefore examine the evidence in the light of all the known surrounding circumstances and the inherent probabilities in order to establish the true intention of the taxpayer. Sometimes a taxpayer will acquire an asset with what has been termed 'mixed intention'; that is to say, with the intention of holding it with some degree of permanence should this turn out to be the prudent thing to do, or of selling it in order to reap quick profits in the event of a reasonably quick rise in its value

> enabling him to do so. Where the purposes or intentions with which a taxpayer acquires an asset are mixed, it is necessary to determine the dominant purpose with which the asset was acquired. If one purpose can be said to have been dominant, and the other merely incidental to that dominant purpose, the dominant purpose will prevail in determining the nature of the asset. If, on the other hand, it is not possible to say that one purpose was dominant, then the taxpayer will have failed in discharging the onus of proving the asset to be a capital asset.

I trust that the contents of the above paragraph will enable my readers to appreciate my point of view when I repeat that I stand in awe of the hold that Inland Revenue has over the taxpayer. With regard to taxation, the latter is guilty until proved innocent. As the judgment quoted phrases it: '*The burden of proving the intention with which an asset was acquired, and of its nature, is upon the taxpayer.*' And a heavy burden it is, too.

The judgment goes on to consider an essential element, namely the length of time for which the asset is held:

> Factors such as the length of time for which the asset is held, and the number of transactions entered into by the taxpayer with regard to assets of that particular kind, may be of importance, but contrary to the popular belief, they are not conclusive. In other words, the fact that an asset is held for a long period of time is merely *prima facie* indicative of the fact that it was acquired by the shareholder to hold with some degree of permanence, but it does not necessarily mean that. Conversely, the fact that it is sold after a short period of time does not mean that it was therefore acquired for a profit-making purpose. Where a taxpayer enters into a number of transactions with, for example, shares involving the buying and selling of shares, this again will generally be indicative of a scheme of profit-making, but not necessarily so.
>
> The final observation which I must make relevant to this case is the following: It is possible where a taxpayer is, what I might call, involved in the share market, and buys and sells shares, his intention with regard to different shares may differ. In other words, the mere facts that he is as it were, dealing in shares quoted on the Stock Exchange, does not mean that all the shares he acquired and sells are either necessarily treated as capital or treated as revenue-producing. It is necessary to look at the purpose for which the taxpayer acquires each particular counter, and the circumstances under which he comes to sell that particular counter. As I have said, the legal principles involved present no difficulty. What is, however, of far greater difficulty is the application of the facts to the law.

5.7 The concept of the taxpayer's 'ipse dixit'

The literal translation of the Latin phrase *ipse dixit* is 'he himself has said it' and the phrase will be come across in matters relating to tax law. Once a taxpayer has entered the witness box, of course at the express invitation of Inland Revenue, his utterances under oath thereafter are referred to as his *ipse dixit*. In other words, the taxpayer himself has said it, with the tacit addition of 'under oath'.

In the judgment of *Friedman*, J quoted in 5.6 we read the following:

> The burden of proving the intention with which an asset was acquired, and of its nature, is upon the taxpayer, and this burden must be discharged by him on a balance of probability. Very often the taxpayer may have no clear idea as to his intention. His recollection may be uncertain and it may be faulty, and more often than not what he says in the witness box to have been his intention is more the product of reconstruction than of positive recollection. The Court must therefore examine the evidence in the light of all the known surrounding circumstances and inherent probabilities in order to establish the true intention of the taxpayer.

This evidence of the taxpayer, relating to his purported intentions in acquiring the assets under investigation, will be given in his *ipse dixit*. The manner in which the Court views the latter, as well as the weight attached to it, is expressed well by *Miller*, J in *ITC* 1185 35 SATC 122:

> It is no difficult matter to say that an important factor is: what was the taxpayer's intention when he bought the property? It is often very difficult, however, to discover what his true intention was.
>
> It is necessary to bear in mind in that regard that the *ipse dixit* of the taxpayer as to his intent and purpose should not lightly be regarded as decisive. It is the function of the court to determine on an objective review of all the relevant facts and circumstances what the motive, purpose and intention of the taxpayer were. Not the least important of the facts will be the course of conduct of the taxpayer in relation to the transaction in issue, the nature of his business or occupation and the frequency or otherwise of his past involvement or participation in similar transactions.
>
> The facts in regard to those matters will form an important part of the material from which the court will draw its own inferences against the background of the general human and business probabilities.
>
> This is not to say that the court will give little or no weight to what the taxpayer says his intention was, as is sometimes contended in argument on behalf of the Secretary in cases of this nature. The taxpayer's evidence under oath and that of his witnesses must necessarily be given full consideration and the credibility of the witnesses must be assessed as in any other case which comes

before the court. But direct evidence of intent and purpose must be weighed and tested against the probabilities and the inferences normally to be drawn from the established facts.

5.8 Résumé

I stated earlier that my aim is to show an annual increase of some 40% in the price of all shares purchased by a correctly operating Stock Exchange participant.

Viewed in terms of the accounting principle of the pre-tax return on capital employed, this figure of 40% per annum will be judged to be very high. Viewed in terms of the *after-tax* return on capital employed, this figure soars to extreme heights. An after-tax return on capital employed of 40% is accomplished by only a very small minority of companies.

It is no wonder, then, that Inland Revenue wishes to make absolutely certain that the Stock Exchange participant achieving this goal is fully entitled to retain his accruals without the normal intervention of that item termed 'taxation'.

Through the Income Tax Act Inland Revenue has permitted the Stock Exchange investor to retain his gains intact, subject to the stringent proviso that they represent what are termed 'accruals of a capital nature'. In all honesty we must acknowledge that this is a magnanimous gesture on the part of Inland Revenue. In only a few countries do capital gains still completely escape taxation. Thus it is expected of a successful Stock Exchange investor that he will obey implicitly, honestly and at all times the requirements laid down by Inland Revenue with regard to the definition 'accrual of a capital nature'. The first of these requirements is that the asset in question must be capable of being defined as a 'capital asset'. As shown in chapter 4, this means that the shareholder must not have acquired his shares with the prime intention of resale at a profit. In support of this, the shareholder is required to disclose the actual intention with which he acquired his shares. This is the second requirement imposed by Inland Revenue on the correctly operating shareholder, and an answer which will satisfy Inland Revenue requires rather detailed knowledge of tax law.

For this reason this aspect became the subject matter of chapters 4 and 5. Many readers may think that I have gone into too much depth and detail in these chapters. I assure them that in order to retain their profits of as high as 40% per annum, the detail offered represents the bare minimum.

As long as he does not sell his shares, Inland Revenue is completely happy with our shareholder achieving his annual gains. At the time of sale, however, *events take a completely different turn*. Once again in all honesty I must state that this is only to be expected. Inland Revenue wishes to make absolutely certain that the shareholder is fully entitled to retain *his now realised profits* without the intervention of taxation.

The one complicating feature here for the shareholder is that in all matters of this type, according to South African tax law he is guilty until proved innocent. This is actually a horrendous state of affairs. In practice it means that Inland Revenue is entitled to regard what our shareholder asserts are accruals of a capital nature as accruals of the opposite, and hence revenue, type. Thus these represent income and are added to the shareholder's disclosed taxable income, and accordingly assessed. The shareholder is obligated to settle this conventionally greatly increased assessment, with all the degrees of financial discomfort this normally entails. Only then may he appeal against what he considers an incorrect view on the part of Inland Revenue. In so doing, he may have to go to considerable financial expense.

It is to make the shareholder aware of these occurrences that I have gone into such detail. My intention is to show him the paths he is legally obligated to follow should he wish to remain immune from Inland Revenue's permitted searchlights. Therefore, instead of regarding these contents as excessively detailed, my readers should now be asking about further aspects of tax case law to expand their knowledge, and hence increase the security of their share purchases and sales. Chapter 6 continues the awareness process by discussing the manner in which the sales of shares is accomplished.

6

Assiduously avoiding a scheme of profit-making

6.1 Introduction

This chapter is the third in which the fundamental topic of discussion is the wrath of Inland Revenue which might be incurred by a not-so-well-informed shareholder when the time comes for him to sell part or all of his shares.

The aim of these three chapters is to convert his status from 'not-so-well-informed' to 'more elite'. To this end, chapter 5 offered important judgments of the Appellate Division. Some of the dicta enunciated therein may seem quite clear to the reader. However, some are sufficiently subtle and far-reaching to make full appreciation thereof necessitate considerable pensive concentration after the first reading.

One such aspect is the phrase 'a scheme for profit-making'. This chapter devotes much attention to this topic.

6.2 A fundamental judgment

The most fundamental judgment which I favour is that in the 1975 case[5] of *Secretary of Inland Revenue v Trust Bank of Africa Ltd.* Here *Botha*, JA states the most basic viewpoint required in the following form:

> The question whether the profits realised on the sale of an asset constituted a revenue or a capital accrual depended upon whether the purchase, holding and sale of the asset were steps in a scheme of profit-making, that is to make a profit by the resale of the asset at an enhanced price, or whether the sale constituted the realisation of a capital asset acquired and held for purposes other than such a profit-making scheme.

The essential sentence here is '. . . acquired and held for purposes *other than* such a profit-making scheme'.

Due scrutiny will reveal that the majority of what may be termed the intricate and complicated contests between Inland Revenue and taxpayers which have occupied the intense concentration of the Appellate Division concern the sale of tracts of land. In such a case the complicating feature for the taxpayer invariably revolves around the clause accentuated above, namely '. . . acquired and held for purposes other than such a profit-making scheme'. Why, for example, in the greater majority of cases, would the taxpayer acquire a bare and undeveloped piece of land? What other purpose could there be in such a situation, since there is no return in the form of an annual income to be derived from it?

A further complication in this undeveloped land example concerns the steps required upon its ultimate sale. If the area encompassed is sufficiently large to permit the development of a township, as invariably proves to be the case, a considerable amount of advance planning is called for. Roads have to be planned, sewerage and storm-water drains have to be designed, and consultants have to be engaged to attend to the sales aspects. In my humble opinion, as a mere mathematician, it proves exceptionally difficult to meet the challenge posed by the '. . . held for purposes *other than* such a profit-making scheme' phrase.

It is possibly for this prime motivation that the exceedingly comprehensive dictum, which I have termed the '*crossing the Rubicon*' dictum, was enunciated as follows by *Holmes*, JA in the 1975 case[4] of *Natal Estates Ltd v Secretary of Inland Revenue*:

> In deciding whether a case is one of realising a capital asset or of carrying on a business or embarking upon a scheme of selling land for profit, one must think one's way through all of the particular facts of each case. Important considerations include, *inter alia*, the intention of the owner, both at the time of buying the land and when selling it (for his intention may have changed in the interim); the objects of the owner, if a company; the activities of the owner in relation to his land up to the time of deciding to sell it in whole or in part; the light which such activities throw on the owner's *ipse dixit* as to intention; where the owner subdivides the land, the planning, extent, duration, nature, degree, organisation and marketing operations of the enterprise, and the relationship of all this to the ordinary commercial concept of carrying on a business or embarking on a scheme for profit.
>
> These considerations are not individually decisive and the list is not exhaustive. From the totality of the facts one enquires whether it can be said that the owner had crossed the Rubicon and gone over to the business, or embarked upon a scheme, of selling such land for profit, using the land as his stock-in-trade.

I consider this enunciation to be magnificently comprehensive in detailing the aspects which are to be taken into account in deciding whether or not the taxpayer has embarked upon a profit-making scheme.

6.3 The essential difference between shares and undeveloped land

The reader may feel that I am being unnecessarily stupid in this matter. Obviously he is aware of the differences between his shares and a piece of undeveloped land. On the other hand, however, there may be some features which he has overlooked, and for the sake of completeness I offer the following discussion.

Possibly the cardinal difference between these two types of asset relates to *the ease with which shares may be acquired and sold*. Unlike the purchase and disposal of land, which is usually associated with legal difficulties, the purchase of shares may be accomplished in as short a time as an hour. The same applies to their disposal.

Despite this tremendous difference, however, Inland Revenue's bright searchlight focuses on the shareholding taxpayer in exactly the same manner as it does on the landowner. In fact, it is because of the simplicity and speed with which the shareholder can dispose of his shares once he has chosen to do so that Inland Revenue's searchlight beams even more brightly and focuses even more intently on him than on the landowner.

The second essential difference between the two assets, and one which acts in favour of the shareholder, concerns the answer to Inland Revenue's enquiry of '. . . acquired and held for purposes other than such a profit-making scheme'. The choice of a share as an asset according to the laws in chapter 3 will always enable the owner to achieve the highly desirable characteristic of *an annual return on his invested funds in the form of dividend income*. This will pacify Inland Revenue in no small measure concerning its enquiry of '. . . held for purposes other than such a profit-making scheme'.

Despite these two major differences, the *crossing the Rubicon* dictum of *Holmes*, JA still applies in each and every aspect of its detailed enunciation to our shareholder as and when he decides to sell his shares.

6.4 Actual situations: Alan, Bertie and Cyril

I stated in 4.8 that the intricacies of Inland Revenue versus the taxpayer shareholder can be lengthy, subtle and often apparently illogical at first sight.

I will now detail certain situations which have actually occurred in order to amplify my outlook as stated above. Rather than refer to them impersonally and impractically as A, B and C, I will call our shareholders Alan, Bertie and Cyril.

These persons all bought their shares some *five years* prior to the October 1987 bull market peak on the Johannesburg Stock Exchange. Each took great pains to comply with the requirements laid down in chapters 3 and 4 here, so that the classification 'capital asset' could be awarded to their shares.

In July 1987 they were all sufficiently erudite to appreciate the existence of a rampant bull market on the Stock Exchange. However, each acted in a different manner in response to this knowledge.

Alan decided to dispose of all his shares in July 1987. He was sufficiently confident of his use of the '*to the best advantage*' dictum of 5.3 to foresee no difficulties with Inland Revenue over his actions. Let us revise the pertaining dictum of *Wessels*, JA to verify Alan's confidence regarding his transaction. It is that:

> Every person who invests his surplus funds in land or stock or any other asset is entitled to realise such asset to the best advantage and to accommodate the asset to the exigencies of the market in which he is selling.

The rapid pace at which his share prices were rising conformed to the situation described above of realising an asset 'to the best advantage and to accommodate the asset to the exigencies of the market in which he is selling'.

Alan took his realised funds and retired from the Stock Exchange. Upon his full, honest and accurate disclosure to Inland Revenue of his actions, accompanied by a lengthy and detailed memorandum explaining the reason for his acquisition and subsequent sale of the shares, Alan was able to sleep in peace and enjoy the fruits of his successful Stock Exchange investment. He was immune from Inland Revenue's searchlight.

Bertie, on the other hand, acted differently. Like Alan, he sold his high priced shares in July 1987, but *decided to purchase other shares which were still offering good value despite the bull market progress*. In other words, he realised his profits on his initial share purchases made five years earlier and then proceeded to use these funds to purchase other shares. *What is termed a 'switch' thus took place*. All this took place in July 1987. In September 1987 Bertie came to the conclusion that even these new shares were far too highly priced, and proceeded to sell them.

What was the attitude of Inland Revenue to Bertie's course of action here? I leave the reader to cogitate on the intricacies of this question while I relate Cyril's story.

Like Alan, Cyril realised that the high prices of his shares could not be justified and he sold all of them and retired from the Stock Exchange, taking his profits with him. However, he remained interested in the further progress of the Stock Exchange. To his chagrin, he saw that the prices of his shares, now sold, continued to rise. From the date of sale to September a rise of some 30% occurred. Finally Cyril could stand it no more, and *re-entered the market* in mid-September, purchasing shares which still reflected some value, although they did not comply with my nine laws. He was sufficiently cool-headed and knowledgeable *to dispose of these new shares* in mid-October, prior to the crash on 27 October.

I ask my readers to place themselves in the position of Inland Revenue in the case of Cyril, and to indicate what Inland Revenue's subsequent actions would be.

6.5 Cyril's case: a blatant example of a scheme of profit-making

I will deal with Cyril's situation first, since it is far simpler than Bertie's. This simplicity arises out of the fact that Cyril's behaviour in re-entering an already steeply climbing market is without doubt *a blatant case of a scheme of profit-making*. This is the first example depicting what Inland Revenue envisages when its wrath is incurred by a taxpayer entering into a scheme of profit-making. There are not even the normal shades of grey which are inevitably used to try to excuse the taxpayer's errant behaviour. Cyril has erred, and there is no doubt whatever on this score, for the following reasons.

In assessing the merits or otherwise of Inland Revenue's supposed case against an allegedly errant Stock Exchange participant, the best procedure is to revert to fundamentals. My approach is: 'When in doubt, always start at the very beginning.'

Chapter 4 indicated that the most fundamental starting point is the taxpayer's answer to the question: 'Was the asset in question acquired with the prime intention of resale at a profit on some future occasion; if not, what was the purpose of the acquisition?' I am of the opinion that not even his very best friend would be convinced if Cyril attempted to answer 'no' to the first part to this question. It is clear that Cyril knowingly and wilfully entered the market the second time in order to reap quick, and hopefully large, profits.

Cyril sold his shares in July 1987 upon realising that at that stage most share prices were illogically high. He would be accurately assessed as having realised his previously defined capital assets 'to the best advantage' by accommodating them to the exigencies of the market into which he was selling. There is no doubt in my mind in this respect. But it is precisely this wise behaviour on Cyril's part in July that finally condemns him for his actions in September. In other words, he is hoisted by his own petard as far as Inland Revenue is concerned.

Having already left an overheated market, how could Cyril possibly explain to Inland Revenue, or even attempt to offer some acceptable reason for, his re-entry one month later?

I have an explanation to offer for what must appear to be completely irrational behaviour on Cyril's part. It concerns the psychological character traits of many Stock Exchange participants. The average Stock Exchange investor hopes and prays that the shares he purchases will begin to rise in price from the very moment of purchase. This is a reasonable request. However, when he sells shares, this same average Stock Exchange investor fervently hopes and prays that *the price will drop immediately*.

I find this attitude somewhat unreasonable. As a portfolio manager, however, I have to admit that only extremely rarely do I come across a client who accepts with good grace the increase in the price of a share which I have recently sold on his behalf. The fact that there were very good and logical reasons for selling his share, for example an unjustifiably high price due to excessive exuberance on the part of prospective buyers regarding its potential, does not concern him. The share went up after the sale; why did I not anticipate this turn of affairs? It is as if his self-image has been dented. As far as this type of shareholder is concerned, he must buy at the very bottom and then sell at the very top. Once I have been able to calm him down, which is not very easy to do I tell him the anecdote of the sign appearing in an Irish fire station: 'All fire-engines are to be checked 24 hours before a fire'!

Unfortunately, Cyril was one of the ardent Stock Exchange participants whose very self-image depends to a large extent on being able to foretell accurately future movements on the market. For him to sell and then observe a price increase as large as the 30% which occurred overall between July and September 1987, was more than he could bear. The reader may find it hard to believe that this type of personality has virtually no control over his actions in the event of such a blow to his self-image. If the market is still rising, whether justifiably or not, he just has to be there to partake in the spoils.

I am able to speak with some authority on this subject as a result of my personal experiences as a portfolio manager during the hectic months between July and October 1987. I had become perturbed by many of the large and completely unjustified share price increases that were occurring. Increases of 30% in one month, and in particular this 30% in one week, were being regarded as the norm.

However not all shares were to be treated in this hurricane manner. There were still some, admittedly by far in the minority, which offered good value even in July 1987. I sold many of my client's shares and switched the proceeds into a share called VADERLAND or its parent company AFRIKAANSE PERS. To quote specific magnitudes, the former was purchased at between 150 and 175 cents, and the latter between 500 and 550 cents.

The shares I had sold continued their illogical climb at an even greater pace and I was lambasted by some of my clients. I received midnight phone calls to the effect that 'Harry's shares have gone up 20% since you sold mine last week. How dare you do that!'. All my attempts at explaining that the prices were excessive or unacceptably high were to no avail. Apparently I was a useless share advisor.

VADERLAND and AFRIKAANSE PERS duly rose to maxima of 240 cents and 680 cents respectively at the market peak, at which prices, surprisingly, they could still be regarded as not being overvalued. Then came the crash on 27 October 1987.

One year after this date, VADERLAND was at 130 cents and AFRIKAANSE PERS at 370 cents. Financial results had appeared in the interim which indicated that these prices could only be classified as heavily pessimistic. Yet no one had the courage to buy at that stage, despite the logic of the situation. To cut a long story short, at the time of writing this chapter, that is August 1989, VADERLAND stands at 240 cents and AFRIKAANSE PERS at 750 cents.

The clients who left me, explaining their course of action in no uncertain terms regarding their possession of their now lowered VADERLAND and AFRIKAANSE PERS shares, have not had the grace or courage to contact me now that these prices are at record highs once again. The trials and tribulations of a portfolio manager are great indeed!

6.6 Bertie's solution: the concept of an 'ipse scripsit'

Bertie's case is not a clear-cut case. There is one recommendation I am able to make, however, which will assist him in persuading Inland Revenue to view his actions in a favourable light. This concerns a new concept which I call the taxpayer's *ipse scripsit*.

We discussed the meaning of the legal term 'the taxpayer's *ipse dixit*' at length in 5.7. It was seen that the literal meaning of *ipse dixit* is 'he himself has said', and that this refers to the taxpayer's verbal utterances while in the unenviable position of the witness box.

Now I propose a new concept which could help the taxpayer to avoid the horror of the witness box. It is the *ipse scripsit*, the literal translation of which is 'he himself has written'. The *ipse scripsit* can be of immeasurable benefit to a taxpayer in the circumstances in which Bertie found himself.

Realising that his shares were overpriced in July 1987, Bertie switched into those shares which still represented good value at that stage. In particular, he chose VADERLAND and AFRIKAANSE PERS. Bertie should then have informed Inland Revenue of this switch in his share portfolio, giving at great length and in all the necessary detail his precise reasons for this course of action. Bertie was knowledgeable enough to realise that the prices of his now sold shares were unacceptably high, and he was sufficiently erudite to calculate that his new shares did not suffer from this drawback and represented good value at the time.

All this he should have submitted in writing to Inland Revenue, together with his normal tax return for the year ended February 1988. The more detailed and well-reasoned this memorandum to Inland Revenue, the greater his chances of receiving a benevolent attitude towards what can only be termed a switch upon a clear and quantitative appraisal of the Stock Exchange as it stood at that time. If the dividend yields or earnings yields of his new acquisitions could convince Inland Revenue of the logic of his course of action, Bertie would stand a good chance of the whole transaction, from the very beginning to its final profit-taking in October 1987, being regarded as merely the realisation of a capital asset to best advantage, accommodating the asset in question to the exigencies of the market into which he was selling.

Such is the value of an *ipse scripsit*, in other words a lengthy written memorandum explaining in detail a shareholder's actions to Inland

Revenue. A well-reasoned *ipse scripsit* may well avoid the unpleasantness of an *ipse dixit*.

6.7 Tax implications of a well-reasoned share switch

Reference to the relevant case law studies will indicate that instances of share switching come a close second to the sale of non-productive land tracts in occupying the attentions of the Special Income Tax Courts. Therefore, for mathematical and investment reasons share switches warrant detailed discussion.

It is readily admitted that many share switches are blatant instances of the carrying on of a scheme of profit-making. On the other hand, however, it must be admitted equally readily that a number of share switches are carried out only after careful and detailed appraisal on the part of the shareholder to determine that it would quite definitely be to his best advantage to effect a switch. Care must be taken not to tar with the same brush the honest endeavours of the latter situation and the blatant disregard for South African tax law represented by the former situations.

In my opinion, the solution for the knowledgeable shareholder who has just accomplished a switch in his share portfolio is to inform Inland Revenue in considerable detail regarding all the salient features which led him to adopt this course of action. If he is able to justify his actions to himself in writing, he is very likely to be able to convince Inland Revenue, too, that he has not contravened tax law and has not carried out a profit-making scheme.

Conventionally there are two main reasons for effecting a share switch. The first is that the shares of the company concerned have performed too well, and the second, quite surprisingly, is that the company concerned has performed unacceptably badly according to its most recently released financial report. These two completely opposite reasons give rise to the same course of action on the part of the shareholder, namely the sale of the shares involved and the reinvestment of the proceeds into a share whose financial prospects have been quantitatively ascertained to be sound. For reasons now to be discussed, Inland Revenue surely cannot penalise the shareholder in either of these two instances.

Take, first, the case of the share whose price rise has been so excessive that it cannot, under any circumstances, be justified by the shareholder. In such a situation the first indication of an excessive rise is that the share's dividend yield has dropped to a level far below that of the sectoral average. Surely the shareholder, acting '*to his best advantage and accommodating his asset to the exigencies of the market into which he is selling*' is entitled to rid himself, at the prevailing profit, of this low dividend yielder and in its place acquire another, but far higher dividend yielding, share. In so doing he is not carrying out a scheme of profit-making. He is merely protecting the value of his capital investment.

I admit that without the presence of a suitable written and detailed explanation on the part of the shareholder, his intentions in the share switch may be hidden to Inland Revenue. The solution in such instances is obvious: the shareholder must convince Inland Revenue first, of his knowledge of the subject, and second, of his honesty of intention by the submission of his *ipse scripsit* as soon as the circumstances dictate.

In the case of the appearance of a dismal financial report by the company concerned, surely the shareholder is entitled to rid himself of these shares? Once again the profits realised are not the result of the carrying on of a profit-making scheme. The shareholder would far rather that the financial performance of the company was up to scratch – he does not want to sell the share, he is being forced to do so to protect the magnitude of his capital involvement. Once again a suitable explanation to Inland Revenue of the reasons precipitating the sale of his shares will, I am sure, rescue the shareholder. Thus the submission of an *ipse scripsit* can be very advantageous.

6.8 Résumé

Thus far three rather detailed chapters on the implications of South African tax law for the correctly operating shareholder have been compiled. The discussion culminates in the proposition to the shareholder that *he forward an accurately compiled ipse scripsit to Inland Revenue every time that he sells any of his shares.*

It is up to his persuasive abilities to satisfy Inland Revenue in this *ipse scripsit* that he was not carrying on a profit-making scheme. His intention is to prove, both to his own satisfaction and to that of Inland Revenue, that he was merely realising a capital asset to its best advantage by accommodating it to the exigencies of the market into which he was selling.

In the absence of an *ipse scripsit* this task may prove impossible. Using an *ipse scripsit*, he may well accomplish his goal.

7

Compiling an accurate and knowledgeable 'ipse scripsit'

7.1 Introduction

We have reached the cardinal point of chapters 4, 5 and 6, namely that a shareholder who operates correctly will forward to Inland Revenue a detailed written memorandum each time he sells any of his shares. This memorandum is what I call the shareholder's '*ipse scripsit*' (literally 'what he himself has written').

Some readers may be either recalcitrant or unenthusiastic about forwarding such a written document to Inland Revenue. To overcome these attitudes, let me put forward my main standpoint once again. My aim is to produce an annual increase of 40% in the share price. In case my readers do not appreciate the consequences in terms of magnitude of such an annual increase, let me now detail the yearly figures which would occur if a taxpayer were to invest only R1 000.

Sum invested	*End of 1st year*	*End of 2nd year*	*End of 3rd year*
R1 000	R1 400	R1 960	R2 744
	End of 4th year	*End of 5th year*	
	R3 842	R5 378	

In other words, at the end of five years he would possess an amount some 5,4 times his original investment. If this latter was R100 000, his share portfolio would stand at R540 000 after only a five-year term.

Should he attempt to realise this profit by selling his shares, he would stand the very real risk of Inland Revenue beaming its searchlight on an amount of R440 000. If our shareholder were in the upper tax bracket, which is highly likely considering the magnitude of his original investment, *he would stand to lose some R200 000 of his realised profits if he were unable to convince Inland Revenue suitably.*

What exactly do I mean by the word 'suitably' here? The answer to this question was the focus of the last three chapters. Being of such importance to the shareholder's financial well-being, the compilation of an accurate and knowledgeable *ipse scripsit* is the focus of this chapter.

In very simple, pragmatic terms, the necessity of a detailed *ipse scripsit* is to perform the vital role of saving the shareholder a considerable sum of money. I trust that my readers' feelings of recalcitrance or unenthusiasm have now evaporated!

7.2 The shareholder's cardinal aim

The previous three chapters have led my readers rather slowly along what may to some have been regarded as a rather laborious tax law path. Now the crux of these chapters must be stated quite unambiguously and incontrovertibly: a correctly operating shareholder simply wishes Inland Revenue to regard any sales of shares by him from time to time *in terms of the dictum of 'to the best advantage'* of 5.3. Very bluntly and directly, this is the essence of chapters 4, 5 and 6 dealing with the intricacies of South African tax law for the participant on the Stock Exchange.

The expression of this important dictum which I particularly like is possibly its earliest enunciation, namely the 1928 judgment of *Wessels*, JA in the *Stott* case.[3] This was given in 5.3 as:

> Every person who invests his surplus funds in land or stock or any other asset is entitled to realise such asset to the best advantage and to accommodate the

> asset to the exigencies of the market in which he is selling. The fact that he does so cannot alter what is an investment of capital into a trade or business for earnings profits.

A re-statement of this 'to the best advantage' dictum was given 47 years later in the following form by *Holmes*, JA in the 1975 *Natal Estates* case:[4]

> It is undoubtedly correct that if, on the facts of a given case, the most that can be said is that the taxpayer was merely realising a capital asset to the best advantage, the proceeds do not become part of his gross income.

Thus the shareholder who has sold his shares wishes Inland Revenue to adopt the point of view that he was 'merely realising a capital asset to the best advantage' and 'accommodating the asset to the exigencies of the market in which he [was] selling'.

That he is capable of expressing his wish so succinctly does not automatically mean, however, that the shareholder will persuade Inland Revenue with similar ease. On the contrary, because of the large sums conventionally involved, Inland Revenue makes the path the shareholder has to follow in order to accomplish his aim a very tortuous one, as the following sections illustrate.

7.3 What is a 'capital asset'?

In order to succeed in his claim that he is 'merely realising a capital asset', the taxpayer must be quite sure as to what a capital asset actually is. Relevant scrutiny will indicate that this has occupied the attention of the Appellate Division for many years. The definition I like is that given by *Corbett*, JA in the 1978 *Elandsheuwel Farming* case[2] in the judgment reported in 5.5:

> In contrast to this, the sale of an asset, acquired with a view to holding it either in a non-productive state or in order to derive income from the productive use thereof and in fact so held, constitutes a realisation of fixed capital and the proceeds an accrual of a capital nature.

From this we glean that a capital asset is one which is 'acquired with a view to holding it either in a non-productive state or in order to derive income from the productive use thereof, and in fact so held'.

A confirmatory viewpoint emerges from the judgment quoted in 6.2 by *Botha*, JA in the 1975 *Trust Bank* case.[5] Here we read that a capital asset is one which is '. . . acquired and held for purposes other than such a profit-making scheme'.

The reader will recognise that I have combined these dicta in the fundamental question which I put to the incumbent shareholder as early as 4.6, namely:

> *Was the asset in question acquired with the prime intention of resale at a profit on some future occasion? If not what was the purpose of the acquisition?*

Thus it becomes apparent that the emphasis is on the *intention* behind the shareholder's acquisition.

7.4 The difficulties now faced by the shareholder

The declaration of his intention at the time of purchase is obviously a nebulous one on the part of the shareholder. In other words, it may be described as a very 'wishy-washy' affair. He may declare, for example, that he acquired his shares with the prime intention of holding them, *whereas his subsequent actions prove otherwise.*

Thus it would appear that a mere statement *purporting to represent his intention of acquisition will not suffice to convince Inland Revenue.* The shareholder will have to attempt to convince the latter by accentuating the second half of the dictum of *Botha*, JA, namely '. . . and held for purposes *other than* such a profit-making scheme'. This is where the concept of the shareholder's annual return in the form of dividend income of suitable magnitude proves important.

Now we come to the prime complicating feature in this connection. In terms of the Income Tax Act, *the onus is on the shareholder to convince Inland Revenue that his shares constitute a capital asset.* Thus here not only do we have the nebulous concept of the shareholder's intention at acquisition, but the onus is on him to persuade Inland Revenue suitably.

The judgment of *Friedman*, J given in 5.4 pinpoints this difficulty well:

> The burden of proving the intention with which an asset was acquired, and of its nature, is upon the taxpayer, and this burden must be discharged by him on a balance of probability. The taxpayer's own evidence as to his intention is of course important, but it is by no means decisive. Very often the taxpayer may have no clear idea as to his intention. His recollection may be uncertain and it may be faulty, and more often than not what he says in the witness box to have been his intention is more the product of reconstruction than of positive recollection. The Court must therefore examine the evidence in the light of all the known surrounding circumstances and the inherent probabilities in order to establish the true intention of the taxpayer.

Just in case the reader missed the important words 'in the witness box', let me stress them now. It is primarily to avoid this horrendous occurrence that submission of an accurately compiled and knowledgeable *ipse scripsit* is recommended in this text. In other words, an adequate *ipse scripsit* will avoid the uncomfortable occurrence of an *ipse dixit*.

Confirmation that the Court will not easily accept the shareholder's *purported* intention of the acquisition of his shares is given by the judgment of *Miller*, J quoted in 5.7. Although the asset acquired in this instance was property, the dictum is of general application. We read:

> It is no difficult matter to say that an important factor is: what was the taxpayer's intention when he bought the property? It is often very difficult, however, to discover what his true intention was.
>
> It is necessary to bear in mind in that regard that the *ipse dixit* of the taxpayer as to his intent and purpose should not lightly be regarded as decisive. It is the function of the court to determine on an objective review of all the relevant facts and circumstances what the motive, purpose and intention of the taxpayer were. Not the least important of the facts will be the course of conduct of the taxpayer in relation to the transaction in issue, the nature of his business or occupation and the frequency or otherwise of his past involvement or participation in similar transactions.
>
> The facts in regard to those matters will form an important part of the material from which the court will draw its own inferences against the background of the general human and business probabilities.

The magnificent euphemism contained in the phrase 'against the background of the general human and business probabilities' should be noted.

I am requesting the correctly operating participant on the Stock Exchange to be completely honest, first with himself and second with

Inland Revenue, when he commits to writing his intention with regard to the acquisition of his shares. He is not going to be allowed to escape with impunity any transgression of this honesty.

The one saving grace in this regard is the dictum of '*foreseeing the possibility*' of *Friedman*, J, which I offered in 5.6. This important dictum reads as follows:

> The fact that, in order to establish an asset to be of a capital nature, the taxpayer must show that he acquired it with the intention to hold it, does not mean that at the time the taxpayer acquired the asset he must have excluded any thought of possibly selling it in future at a profit. Very often (indeed it is perhaps usual even where a taxpayer acquires a capital asset), he foresees the possibility that with the ravages of inflation and the erosion of money, that asset will grow in value in the sense that its monetary value will increase and that he may one day, therefore, be able to sell it at a price greater than the price at which he acquired it. The fact that the taxpayer, in acquiring the asset foresees these possibilities, will not in itself render the asset thereby something other than capital.'

The shareholder is entitled to make full use of this potent dictum in the compilation of his *ipse scripsit*.

To summarise the progress we have made thus far, our correctly operating shareholder has acquired his shares and should be in a position to state quite openly and honestly in writing precisely what his intentions with regard to this acquisition are. Once again I remind our shareholder of the potent dictum of *Botha*, JA, namely '. . . acquired and held for purposes *other than* such a profit-making scheme'.

7.5 The shareholder now wishes to sell his previously defined capital asset

The time has come when our shareholder, previously intent on holding his shares and thus complying with the definition of a capital asset, wishes to sell them. That this change of intention is permitted in law has been discussed in 5.2. The '*something more*' dictum of *Trollip*, JA from the 1978 *Elandsheuwel Farming* case[2] is important here:

> Of course, every decision by an owner to dispose of an asset held as a capital asset does involve a change of intention; hitherto his intention has been to retain it as such; now he changes that intention by deciding to dispose of it.

> According to the above-mentioned *dicta* a mere change of intention of that kind does not *per se* subject any resultant gain to tax; something more is required for that to happen. That additional factor is usually something indicating that the disposal is in reality in pursuance of some trade or business or scheme for making profit. The intervention of such an additional factor may be indicated by the circumstances surrounding the change of intention or in the way in which it was manifested or carried out.

In other words the change of intention will be permitted, provided that the disposal is in reality not in pursuance of some trade or business or scheme for making profit. *The shareholder wishing to sell his shares must therefore be in a position to explain to Inland Revenue exactly why this wish has arisen.*

This is the stage at which the shareholder is required *by quantitative evidence alone* to prove to Inland Revenue that, in accordance with the dictum '*to the best advantage*' of *Wessels*, JA in the 1928 *Stott* case[3] as discussed in 7.2, he was merely realising 'such asset to the best advantage and to accommodate the asset to the exigencies of the market in which he is selling'. Once again I repeat the stringent condition that *it is specifically and only by due quantitative calculation and interpretation* that the shareholder can expect to be granted the benefits of this dictum by Inland Revenue.

In simpler language, this means that the shareholder must know precisely *why he is doing what he is doing* regarding the sale of his shares. If he does not, Inland Revenue will most certainly and with justification penalise any profits. In all honesty we ask the question 'Did the ignorant or errant shareholder possibly think otherwise?' First, after-tax returns on the taxpayer's invested funds of as large as 40% per annum must most definitely be earned, and second, once obtained these must be validated and justified to avoid that all-powerful and well-focused searchlight which Inland Revenue is entitled to use to very good effect.

7.6 Using Posel's nine laws to discharge the onus of 'to the best advantage'

The use of my nine laws will provide the knowledgeable shareholder with virtually all he needs in his quantitative attempts to invoke the dictum 'to the best advantage'. This will occur as follows.

The shareholder will want to sell his shares for one of the following three reasons:

- ☐ He wishes to realise his profits to meet a recent financial commitment. In this case he is *withdrawing* his funds from the Stock Exchange, and upon an adequate explanation of this situation to Inland Revenue, and provided the frequency of such profit realisations is all above board, he will normally be treated benevolently by the powerful searchlight.

- ☐ The shareholder finds that his shares are over-priced. In order to have established this finding he will have had to use at least four of my laws. Since this is a quantitative area of research and explanation, once again Inland Revenue will accept his reasons for the realisation of his profits subject to a logical and well-motivated *ipse scripsit*.

- ☐ The shareholder finds through studying the most recent financial results of the company concerned, that his shares therein do not satisfy some of my nine laws, whereas previously they did. If this had not been the case, he would most certainly not have bought those shares in the first place. Once again, upon this quantitative explanation Inland Revenue will adopt a benevolent stance, since obviously the shareholder is quite entitled to express his disappointment in his company's performance. This latter is subject to the express stipulation that the shareholder is able to validate his standpoint accurately and comprehensively.

On these quantitative grounds the shareholder is entitled to claim use of '*to the best advantage*'. His accurately documented memorandum will also satisfy the important stipulations of that all-embracing '*crossing the Rubicon*' dictum. As I explained in 6.2, it is this latter which decides whether or not the shareholder's sale of his shares is 'a case of realising a capital asset or of carrying on a business or embarking upon a scheme of selling for profit'.

To me the most stringent pronouncement of *Holmes*, JA in the 1975 *Natal Estates* case[4] is contained in the following sentence:

> Important considerations include, inter alia, the intention of the owner, both at the time of buying the land and *when selling it* (for his intention may have changed in the interim).

7.7 Conclusion

In order to enjoy his sojourn on the Stock Exchange, the correctly operating investor should have as possibly his first priority the endeavour to make and stay friends with Inland Revenue. To many readers this bland statement may come as more than a surprise. Chapters 4 to 7 inclusive provide sufficient material to sustain this very necessary friendship. Long may it last.

PART 2

Adding the desirable character trait of patience

8

Movement in AUTOQUIP'S share price after the interim results

8.1 Introduction

Having dealt comprehensively in chapters 4 to 7 with the important but oft-neglected topic, the taxation of realised profits on share transactions, we turn, once again, to a consideration of the AUTOQUIP share.

Chapter 3 gives a detailed discussion of my reasons for purchasing this share immediately after the appearance of its interim results on 13 March 1989. The present chapter reports on the price movements that occurred in response to AUTOQUIP's performance as reflected in these results.

It is extremely important that a reader who has never before experienced such a price response be given a detailed account of the daily changes occurring during the first week after the publication of the financial results. A discussion of the outlook of the various buyers and sellers who appear on the scene provides an interesting view of the ignorance that some shareholders persist in exhibiting. This, then, is the aim of chapter 8.

8.2 The day before the appearance of the interim results: Day −1

As indicated in fig 3.1, the interim results appeared in the financial press on Monday 13 March 1989. It is interesting to examine the movements of the AUTOQUIP share price on the trading day *before* the appearance of these results. The esoteric manner in which this information is presented in the financial press is indicated in table 8.1. I will interpret this rather formidable-looking table step by step for the reader who may not as yet have been exposed to this form of presentation. The table indicates, first, the prices occurring during the operations of Friday 10 March, and second, the changes which occurred over that week. For obvious reasons I shall denote this Friday 'Day −1'.

We commence with a consideration of the three columns just to the right of the name AUTOQUIP which contain the figures 50 55 55. The first of these columns represents the buyers' price at the *end of the day*, the second the sellers' price pertaining, and the third the most important information, namely the price at which the last sale before the close of business was conducted. Thus we know, first, that at the close of business on Friday 10 March 1989 there was a buyer for AUTOQUIP offering a price of 50 cents, second, that there was simultaneously a seller who was asking a price of 55 cents, and third, that the sale conducted was at the seller's price of 55 cents. An important additional piece of information to be obtained herefrom is that it was the seller who ruled the roost – the buyer had to increase his price to meet that of the seller in order to clinch the deal. This is normally a good omen.

Now consider columns four to seven to the right. These contain the figures 55 55 5+ 10%. Column 4 indicates the highest price achieved for AUTOQUIP during that day's trading, column 5 the lowest such price, and column 6 the change the closing price represented over that of the previous day. Hence we are informed that the highest price achieved for AUTOQUIP during trading on Friday 10 March 1989 was 55 cents, as was the lowest price. In other words, all transactions were at the price of 55 cents. This is an increase of 5 cents over the previous closing price, representing a 10% change (column 7).

Now we come to a consideration of the volume of shares traded. The column headed D.V. indicates the daily figure, while that headed W.V.

Table 8.1 Trading figures for Friday 10 March 1989 and for the week ended on this date

P.E.	E.Y.	D.Y.		BUY	SELL	LAST	H	L	D.M.	D.M.%	Y.M.%	D.V.	W.M.%	W.V.
						RETAILERS & WHOLSLRS								
5,2	19,1	5,2	AROMA	43		43				0,0	38,6 –		0,0	
4,6	21,8	8,1	AKJ		50	50				0,0	25,0 +		0,0	
5,2	19.1	8,2	AUTOQIP	50	55	55	55	55	5 +	10,0	15,4 –	36000V	0,0	54200
9,4	10,7	4,3	BERGERS	145		145	145	135	10 +	7,4	20,8 +	20200V	3,6 +	48400
11,9	8,4	3,3	BIDCORP	750		750				0,0	25,0 +		0,0	5000
		10,7	BIDCORP C	550	575	575	575	575		0,0	9,5 +	1000	0,0	4000
5,2	19.2	6,5	BOYMANS	200	220	200	200	200		0,0	11,1 +	5500V	0,0	26300
10,9	9,2	3,1	CASHBIL	220		220	220	220		0,0	10,0 +	2200V	1,4 +	3600
11,6	8,6	4,2	*CLICKS	650		650	650	650	20 +	3,2	16,1 –	14600V	7,4 +	16600
9,8	10,2	4,1	CNAGALO			790	790	790		0,0	79,5 +	500	0,0	10700
4,5	22,1	7,0	CONTRAV	35		38	38	35	3 +	8,6	15,6 –	1600	8,6 +	3360
5,5	18,1	8,3	CURNOW	35	37	36	37	36	1 +	2,9	28,0 –	28000V	9,1 +	39400
4,2	24.0	10,8	DECHOLD		50	53S				0,0	3,6 –		0,0	
3,9	25.7	12,0	DIALMOV		36	35				0,0	12,5 –		2,8 –	5000
2,9	36,0	13,3	DRIVTEC	60	65	60	60	60		0,0	29,4 –	39240	0,0	141713
5,8	17,1	10,3	DROPINN		36	35	35	35	1 –	2,8	12,5 –	600	5,4 –	85800
9,9	10,1	3,4	EDGARS	1700	1750	1750	1750	1750	50 –	2,8	54,3 +	2600V	2,8 –	4300
		3.9	EDGARS CD	1700	2000	1667B				0,0	19,1 +		0,0	
7,7	13,0	4,5	FOCUS	50		50	50	50		0,0	25,0 +	10300V	11,1 +	24500
4,4	22,6	10,0	FLEIMAN	85		85	85	85		0,0	29,2 –	32900V	0,0	141100
13,0	7,7	3,2	FOSCHINI	4900		4850B				0,0	67,2 +		4,3 +	5000
4,6	21,5	5,2	FRASERS	575	585	575	575	575		0,0	36,1 –	80	0,9 +	2980
		16,5	FRASER CD	80		83				0,0	17,0 –		0,0	
4,5	22.0	6,0	FRASCON	240	250	245				0,0	23,4 –		2,1 +	5000
			GARCON	SUS	PEN	DED								
5,7	17,7	7,1	GRESHAM		120	120	120	120		0,0	20,0 +	10000V	0,0	17000
16,7	6,0	5,4	HISCORE	360	370	360	360	360		0,0	52,0 –	16527V	0,0	58054
4,1	24,2	7,8	HOMAKER	77	80	77	77	77		0,0	45,0 –	15670	13,2 +	516154
6,0	16,7	5,0	IBJOFFE		105	100				0,0	11,1 +		0,0	1200
2,8	35.9	5,3	*INTHOLD			625				0,0	13,6 +		0,0	2400
		8,9	INTH 7%CP			520				0,0	8,1 –		0,0	
		17,7	INTH 13CD			485				0,0	15,1 –		0,0	
4,9	20.6	8,0	JAZZ	71		71	71	70	1 +	1,4	52,7 –	4500	11,3 –	48300
4,3	23,4	3,5	KIMET		100	100				0,0	42,9 +		4,8 –	28600
		11,1	KIMET 7%CP			85				0,0	15,0 –		0,0	
		21,7	KIMET 13CD			81				0,0	12,0 –		0,0	
13,2	7,6	3,1	LEFIC	2200	2750	2500	2500	2500		0,0	28,2 +	100	0,0	100
10,6	9,4	4,7	MASCON		168	165				0,0	25,0 –		0,0	
7,5	13,4	6,5	MASHOLD	170		170				0,0	12,8 –		0,0	5400
9,8	10,2	4,6	*METRO		490	490	490	490		0,0	21,6 –	2322	1,0 –	22248
15,5	6,5	2,0	MIDAS	1300	1400	1310	1310	1310		0,0	138,2 +	1000	0,8 +	3700
4,8	20,6	7,5	MILSTAN	80	85	80				0,0	15,8 –		0,0	55100
8,8	11,3	6,1	*O K	1530		1530	1530	1530		0,0	27,5 +	950	2,0 +	4819
15,2	6,6	2,6	PENPIN		200	190	190	190		0,0	72,7 +	900	0,0	33400
9,7	10.3	3,7	PEPGRO		1975	1975				0,0	16,2 +		1,3 –	200
		4,6	PEPGRO 7%			1500				0,0	58,9 +		7,1 +	120
		6,2	PEPGRO 13		2050	1854				0,0	5,8 –		0,0	
9.0	11,1	3,7	*PEPKOR			3700	3700	3700		0,0	23,3 +	700	0,0	3550
		5,2	PEPKOR 7%			2500				0,0	156,4 +		0,0	160
		6,9	PEPKOR 13		3250	3044				0,0	22,1 +		0,0	
9,2	10.9	4,0	PEPSTOR			1300	1300	1300		0,0	11,9 –	100	0,0	1712
33,1	3,0	3,0	PIKWIK	560	570	570	570	570	10 +	1,8	50,0 +	6400V	0,9 –	24500
15,6	6,4	3,0	PICKNPAY	1160	1180	1175	1175	1175	15 +	1,3	51,6 +	12400V	0,0	31100
8,1	12,3	4,6	REGGIES	52		52	52	52	2 +	4,0	22,4 –	11780V	5,5 –	27936
4,7	21,3	9,5	SANLIC	40		40				0,0	20,0 –		0,0	15600
14,2	7,0	4,7	SCOCLIK		215	220S				0,0	32,3 –		2,2 –	1870
8,0	12,5	4,8	*SCORE		825	800	800	800	10 +	1,3	51,5 –	1075	0,0	5650
8,6	11,7	4,6	SHIELD	62	65	65	65	62	3 +	4,8	59,4 –	1400	0,0	13800
13,2	7,6	3,2	SHOPRIT	270	275	270	270	270	10 –	3,6	8,0 +	200	0,0	5900
8,1	12,4	4,7	STORECO	825		825	825	825		0,0	22,2 +	500	0,0	7100
3,4	29,3	12,2	SPECTRUM	45	50	45	45	45		0,0	18,2 –	12000V	0,0	31215
3,8	26.2	6,3	SPITZ		190	175	175	175	15 –	7,9	75,0 +	200V	12,5 –	500
			SPITZ OPT			25				0,0	72,2 –		0,0	
3,1	32,1	11,4	SPRINGTEX	72	85	70B	70	70	15 –	17.6	36.4 –	60400V	22,2 –	173100
5,2	19.2		*STERNS			170				0,0	13,3 +		2,9 –	6100
4,7	21.2	7,0	TARRY	430		430	430	430	10 +	2,4	7,5 +	15000V	2,4 +	74800
8,7	11,5	5,0	TELJOY	240	250	240	240	240		0,0	4,3 +	16300V	0,0	43900
10,2	9.8		TRABILD		55	55				0,0	83,3 +		8,3 –	5000
		13,9	TRABILD P			61				0,0	18,7 –		0,0	
			TRABILD C			53				0,0	6,0 +		0,0	
2,7	37,3	5,3	*TRADGRO	170	175	170	175	170	5 –	2,9	13,3 +	38247V	8,1 –	64458
		14,4	TRADGR PP	90	95	90				0,0	5,3 –		0,0	8844
		16,3	TRADGR CP	200		210	210	210		0,0	5,0 +	7748V	0,0	30248
		9,5	TRGR A7CP	110		110	110	110	10 +	10,0	8,3 –	400V	10,0 +	400
		10,8	TRGR 13CD	175	185	180				0,0	20,0 +		0,0	24200
		9,8	TRGR 100CD	105	200	200				0,0	14,3 +		0,0	
4,6	21,9	9,3	VADEK	43	45	40	43	42	1 +	2,4	21,8 –	3600V	7,5 +	9400
11,9	8,4	2,9	WALHOLD	525	530	525	525	525		0,0	59,1 +	22050V	2,8 +	74950
12,1	8,3	2,7	*WALTONS		550	560	666	560	5 –	0,9	59,4 +	9600	2,8 +	50000
11,0	9,1	3,8	*WOOLTRU	2350	2400	2400	2400	2350	50 +	2,1	81,1 +	7500	4,3 +	17720
11,0	9,1	3,8	*WOOLTRU-A	2350	2400	2400	2400	2350	50 +	2,1	88,2 +	4500	7,9 +	12125
	7,9	4,7	AVERAGE DAYS TRADE TOTALS						R**1331112			VOL		479389

P.E. = price earnings ratio **E.Y.** = earnings yield **D.Y.** = dividend yield **H** = highest price reached during tho day **L** – lowest price reached during the day **D.M** = daily movement **D.V.** – daily volumo **W.V.** – weekly volume of shares traded indicates the weekly traded volume. Thus we see that 36 000 shares changed hands on the Friday in question, while 54 200 were traded throughout the whole week.

The column headed W.M.% indicates the percentage change in share price over the week. This was zero; in other words AUTOQUIP ended the previous week at 55 cents, the same figure at which it ended the week under investigation.

To summarise events for AUTOQUIP during the week immediately preceding the release of its interim results on 13 March 1989, the share price remained at 55 cents and the total weekly volume of 54 200 shares was traded.

The rest of table 8.1 is offered to show the reader the values of the average dividend yield and earnings yield of the RETAILERS AND WHOLESALERS sector as at the close on Friday 10 March 1989. The figures are 4,7% and 7,9% respectively. We recognise AUTOQUIP, with its corresponding 8,2% for the dividend yield and 19,1% for the earnings yield, *to be undervalued* compared with the rest of this sector. This is an important statement, since even before the release of its interim results, the share was undervalued compared with the rest of the sector in which it is housed.

8.3 Events of Day 0: Monday 13 March 1989

I receive my daily financial newspaper at 06h00. On Monday 13 March 1989 I open this newspaper with my early morning tea, to see the interim report for AUTOQUIP for the six months ended 31 December 1988. The financial results as they appear are shown in fig 3.1. The very first piece of information that I focus on is an 81% increase in earnings-per-share over the corresponding period the year before.

Quickly I perform my laws 3 to 9 inclusive, as detailed in chapter 3. This takes some two hours to accomplish. I find that AUTOQUIP fulfills all of these stringent requirements and that the share is worthy of purchase.

Now I bring section 1.5 in its entirety into operation, with the accent on the following specific paragraphs:

> Let us presume that the share in question has satisfied all my nine laws, and thus is a candidate for purchase. I now have to come to grips with the realisation that when I purchase this share, I obtain it from a person who is so dissatisfied with it that he no longer wants to possess it. In other words, my possession is the result of his rejection of the same goods.
>
> Now the ultimate question. Of the two of us, who is right? Obviously we cannot both be correct. I want what he no longer wants. Very succinctly, this is the essence of Stock Exchange entry.
>
> It is at this stage that the attribute of confidence in one's quantitative abilities is either born or enhanced. The prospective investor must now put his money where his brains are. He cannot lean on anyone else; he is on his own now.
>
> The prospective buyer must not only make up his mind, but also have or acquire the ability to make his mind up in a hurry. There may well be other buyers equally enthusiastic about acquiring the very same shares. What does our investor do upon realising that he does not have sole rights to the buying opportunity for his carefully selected share, that there are other equally erudite persons on the scene?

The really magnificently high standard of AUTOQUIP's results as shown in fig 3.1 tends to simplify to a large extent the normally harassing moments described above. I phone my broker at his home and manage to catch him before he leaves for the office. This is just one of the many advantages of our 20-year association.

Table 8.1, to which I would obviously refer, shows me that the previous closing price for AUTOQUIP is 55 cents and can only be described as a ridiculously low price in the light of the results of fig 3.1, and therefore I place my buying order at what is esoterically termed 'at best'. That is, I place no upper price limit on the purchase price that I offer. I calculate the quantity of shares that my present finances are able to support, thank my broker for his assistance and wish him a good day, and pour my second cup of tea.

Now for a rather detailed discussion of a personal nature for the benefit of the newcomer to the Stock Exchange. I have just placed a buying order involving tens of thousands of rands. Do I now pace the floor nervously and wish that I could revoke my decision, which was taken at great speed? Is nailbiting the order of the day?

On this score I am able to reply with a definite 'No'. Either I know what I am doing, or I don't. To support me in the former instance, I applied seven extremely stringent and completely quantitatively based laws prior to my decision to purchase the AUTOQUIP share. Assuming that my arithmetical calculations are accurate, I must now gain the feeling of confidence that a successful participant on the Stock Exchange simply has to acquire if he is to enjoy his operations there. Such enjoyment of one's investment programme prompted me to write this text.

I ask the reader who has never before experienced this feeling of confidence to trust me when I say that it can be achieved, possibly not on his first, second or even third buying mission, but quite definitely thereafter if each of his previous missions has met with success.

I normally experience a feeling of exhilaration and delightful anticipation during the course of a day on which I have placed a buying order with my broker. My readers may consider this to be exaggeration. Surely I feel some tension throughout the day, in view of the amount of finance involved? I can only assure them that exactly the opposite is the case and I feel no tension whatsoever. I may go back and check and re-check my calculations, but once I have confirmed that my calculations are indeed accurate, I experience a delightful sense of expectation and exhilaration.

Around lunch time my broker 'phones. There are six or seven other buyers on the scene and as a result he has been able to purchase only a small portion of my original order. Now for me some rather astounding news: *the price is still 55 cents*. Despite the appearance of financial results of an absolutely first-rate standard, AUTOQUIP's share price remains at its previous level.

Paradoxically, were the price to increase dramatically I would feel relieved because other buyers feel similarly inclined to push up the price in their endeavours to obtain the share. However, the price remains the same and I worry momentarily. Have I made a mistake? Does the seller know more than I do about the AUTOQUIP share? I go over my laws 3 to 9 inclusive once again and as the result of the quantitative reassurance obtained from them, I relax.

At the end of DAY 0 my broker 'phones again. He has obtained only a small portion of my order, but all at 55 cents. I reiterate my intention to complete the outstanding portion, once again at best. What finally fires my enthusiasm is that there were three other buyers on the scene and the selling broker decided to share the AUTOQUIP shares available equally among all buyers. I am finally informed that the volume of trade in the share was 32 500. In other words, each of us obtained 8 000 AUTOQUIP shares, all at 55 cents.

I now ask myself the inevitable question: who on earth would want to sell AUTOQUIP shares on the very day that such magnificent results are published, specifically in the large quantity of 32 500 and at the very low price of 55 cents?

Why do I keep insisting to myself that this price is indeed very low? On the basis of my quantitative assessment of its prevailing dividend yield, in the first instance. On the basis of a dividend of 5,5 cents for the past twelve months, a figure obtained from fig 3.1, the dividend yield is 5,5/55 or 10% of the price of 55 cents. Table 8.1 shows that the average such yield for the sector in which AUTOQUIP is housed is 4,7%. There is no argument or doubt whatsoever in my mind following this calculation: the AUTOQUIP share is incontrovertibly undervalued at the price of 55 cents with the consequent dividend yield of 10% compared with the sector's average figure of 4,7%.

Now I begin to pity the sellers for having disposed of their shares to me at this ridiculously low figure, but quickly I realise that their error is my gain; were it not for their ignorance, I and the other buyers could not have benefited from the situation. Finally, a summary of the complete day's trading is revealed in table 8.2.

8.4 Events of DAY +1: Tuesday 14 March 1989

With only one third of my buying order executed, this day is also one of anticipation and exhilaration. However, there is nothing more for me to do other than wait for information on my broker's progress.

Once again this comes at lunch time. *The price has now climbed to 65 cents, and he has not been able to complete my order*. There are

Table 8.2 Share prices and volumes traded as at the close of Monday 13 March 1989, the day on which AUTOQUIP's interim results appeared in the early morning press

P.E.	E.Y.	D.Y.		BUY	SELL	LAST	H	L	D.M.	D.M.%	Y.M.%	D.V.
						RETAILERS & WHOLSLRS						
4,9	20,5	5,6	AROMA		43	40	40	40	3 –	7,0	42,9 –	9000V
4,6	21,8	8,1	AKJ		50	50				0,0	25,0 +	
5,2	19,1	8,2	AUTOQIP	50	55	55	55	55		0,0	15,4 –	32500V
9,4	10,7	4,3	BERGERS		145	145				0,0	20,8 +	
11,9	8,4	3,3	BIDCORP	750		750	750	750		0,0	25,0 +	1900
		10,7	BIDCORP C	575		575	575	575		0,0	9,5 +	7000
5,0	20,0	6,8	BOYMANS	190	210	192				0,0	6,7 +	
10,9	9,2	3,1	CASHBIL	220		220				0,0	10,0 +	
11,8	8,5	4,1	*CLICKS	660		660	660	660	10 +	1,5	14,8 –	3900V
9,8	10,2	4,1	CNAGALO			790	790	790		0,0	79,5 +	200
4,8	21,0	6,7	CONTRAV	36	40	40	40	40	2 +	5,3	11,1 –	320
5,5	18,1	8,3	CURNOW	36	38	36				0,0	28,0 –	
4,2	24,0	10,8	DECHOLD			53				0,0	3,6 –	
3,9	25,7	12,0	DIALMOV		35	35				0,0	12,5 –	
2,9	35,0	13,3	DRIVTEC	60	63	60	60	60		0,0	29,4 –	23140
5,8	17,1	10,3	DROPINN	35		35	35	35		0,0	12,5 –	5600
9,9	10,1	3,4	EDGARS		1800	1750	1750	1750		0,0	54,3 +	4200V
		3,9	EDGARS CD			1667				0,0	19,1 +	
7,7	13,0	4,5	FOCUS	50	55	50				0,0	25,0 +	
4,7	21,3	9,4	FLEIMAN	87	95	90	90	87	5 +	5,9	26,0 –	61400V
9,9	10,1	4,2	FOSCHINI	4900		4850B				0,0	67,2 +	
4,6	21,5	5,2	FRASERS	575		575	575	575		0,0	36,1 –	100
		16,5	FRASER CD	80	85	83				0,0	17,0 –	
4,5	22,0	6,0	FRASCON	240	250	245				0,0	23,4 –	
			GARCON	SUS	PEN	DED						
5,4	18,4	7,4	GRESHAM		120	115	115	115	5 –	4,2	15,0 +	20000V
17,2	5,8	5,3	HISCORE	360	450	370	370	370	10 +	2,8	50,7 –	3250
4,3	23,3	7,5	HOMAKER	80	90	80	80	77	3 +	3,9	42,9 –	130380V
6,0	16,7	5,0	IBJOFFE		105	100				0,0	11,1 +	
2,8	35,9	5,3	*INTHOLD			625				0,0	13,6 +	
		8,9	INTH 7%CP			520				0,0	8,1 –	
		17,7	INTH 13CD			485				0,0	15,1 –	
4,8	20,9	8,1	JAZZ	68	75	70	70	70	2 +	2,9	53,3 –	3000
4,3	23,4	3,6	KIMET		100	100	100	100		0,0	42,9 +	4000
		11,1	KIMET 7%CP	80		85				0,0	15,0 –	
		21,7	KIMET 13CD	90		81B				0,0	12,0 –	
11,1	9,0	3,8	LEFIC	2500		2750	2750	2750	250 +	10,0	41,0 +	8700V
10,6	9,4	4,7	MASCON			165				0,0	25,0 –	
7,5	13,4	6,5	MASHOLD			170	170	170		0,0	12,8 –	1500V
9,8	10,2	4,6	*METRO	485	495	490	490	490		0,0	21,6 –	220774V
15,5	6,5	2,0	MIDAS	1300	1400	1310				0,0	138,2 +	
4,8	20,6	7,5	MILSTAN	80	85	80				0,0	15,8 –	
9,0	11,2	6,1	*O K	1550	1575	1550	1550	1550	20 +	1,3	29,2 +	2700V
15,2	6,6	2,6	PENPIN		190	190				0,0	72,7 +	
9,7	10,3	3,7	PEPGRO		1950	1975S				0,0	16,2 +	
		4,6	PEPGRO 7%		1600	1500				0,0	58,9 +	
		6,2	PEPGRO 13		2050	1854				0,0	5,8 –	
9,0	11,1	3,7	*PEPKOR		3700	3700				0,0	23,3 +	
		5,2	PEPKOR 7%			2500				0,0	156,4 +	
		6,9	PEPKOR 13		3200	3044				0,0	22,1 +	
9,2	10,9	4,0	PEPSTOR		1300	1300	1300	1300		0,0	11,9 –	100
32,0	3,1	3,1	PIKWIK	540	570	550	560	550	20 –	3,5	44,7 +	3300
15,4	6,5	3,0	PICKNPAY	1160	1175	1160	1175	1160	15 –	1,3	49,7 +	26866V
7,8	12,8	4,8	REGGIES	50	55	50	50	50	2 –	3,8	25,4 –	2688
4.7	21.3	9,5	SANLIC	40	45	40	40	40		0,0	20,0 –	1000
14.2	7.0	4,7	SCOCLIK	200	225	220	220	220		0,0	32,3 –	106523V
8.0	12.5	4.8	*SCORE		800	800				0,0	51,5 –	
8.2	12.3	4.8	SHIELD			62	62	62	3 –	4,6	61,3 –	3000
13.2	7.6	3.2	SHOPRIT	270	275	270				0,0	8,0 +	
8.2	12.2	4.7	STORECO	825	840	835	835	835	10 +	1,2	23,7 +	2000V
3,4	29,3	12,2	SPECTRUM	45		45				0,0	18,2 –	
3,8	26,2	6,3	SPITZ	165	200	175				0,0	75,0 +	
			SPITZ OPT			25				0,0	72,2 –	
3,1	32,1	11,4	SPRINGTEX	75	80	70B				0,0	36,4 –	
5,2	19,2		*STERNS			170				0,0	13,3 +	
4,5	22,0	7,2	TARRY	410	430	414				0,0	3,5 +	
8,7	11,5	5,0	TELJOY	230	240	240	240	240		0,0	4,3 +	900
10,2	9,8		TRABILD	50	58	55	55	56		0,0	83,3 +	50
		13,9	TRABILD P			61				0,0	18,7 –	
			TRABILD C		55	53				0,0	8,0 +	
2,7	37,3	5,3	*TRADGRO	170	175	170	170	170		0,0	13,3 +	13116
		13,7	TRADGR PP	90	95	95	95	95	5 +	5,6	0,0	2000
		16,3	TRADGR CP			210				0,0	5,0 +	
		9,5	TRGR A7CP	110		110	110	110		0,0	8,3 –	18
		10,8	TRGR 13CD	175	185	180				0,0	20,0 +	
		9,8	TRGR 130CD	180	200	200				0,0	14,3 +	
4,6	21,9	9,3	VADEK	43	45	43	43	43		0,0	21,8 –	2500V
11,9	8,4	2,9	WALHOLD	525	550	525	525	525		0,0	59,1 +	2800
12,1	8,3	2,7	*WALTONS			550	550	550		0,0	59,4 +	12600
10,8	9,3	3,9	*WOOLTRU		2375	2353				0,0	77,6 +	
10,8	9,3	3,9	*WOOLTRU-A	2300	2400	2350	2350	2350	3 –	0,1	84,3 +	3500
12.2	8,2	4,9	AVERAGE DAYS TRADE TOTALS						R**2541345		VOL	726525

numerous other buyers present and it may take some time for him to obtain the balance. Do I wish to proceed at this new and increased price of 65 cents? I assure him immediately that I do.

The price of AUTOQUIP has increased from 55 to 65 cents in one morning's trading. *This represents a large percentage increase of 18,2% in only one morning.*

My feelings of exhilaration are justified. My self-image has improved quite dramatically, not because of the finance involved, but purely and simply because I put my money where my brains were, and I have been proved correct. I repeat here what I stated in this regard in chapter 1:

> All in all, then, the purchaser's character trait concerned with accurate decision making under pressure, with rather disastrous consequences should he be proved wrong, is considerably enhanced by correct Stock Exchange investment procedures. But if he is right, and he has the protection of my nine laws in this connection to ensure a high probability of such an occurrence, then the increase in his self-image is so great that it has to be experienced personally to be described.

At the end of the day my broker 'phones to say that he has not been able to complete my order, but now there is only a small amount outstanding. The closing price of AUTOQUIP remains at 65 cents, and this time the large volume of 75 200 shares changed hands.

Once again I ask myself who would be so ignorant as to sell as large a quantity as 75 200 AUTOQUIP shares at the now 'relatively' low price of 65 cents?

The day's trading is summarised in table 8.3.

Table 8.3 Events at the close of Tuesday 14 March. The share price has increased to 65 cents, an 18,2% increase, in only one day. The large volume of 75 200 AUTOQUIP shares has left the hands of their previous and now hapless owners

P.E.	E.Y.	D.Y.		BUY	SELL	LAST	H	L	D.M.	D.M.%	Y M %	D V
						RETAILERS & WHOLSLRS						
4,9	20,5	5,6	AROMA			40				0,0	42,9 –	
4,6	21,8	8,1	AKJ		50	50				0,0	25,0 +	
6,2	16,2	6,9	AUTOQIP	60	70	65	65	65	10 +	18,2	0,0	75200V
9,0	11,1	4,5	BERGERS			140	140	140	5 –	3,4	16,7 +	2500
11,9	8,4	3,3	BIDCORP		750	750				0,0	25,0 +	
		10,7	BIDCORP C			575	575	575		0,0	9,5 +	2000
5,0	20,0	6,8	BOYMANS	190	210	192				0,0	6,7 +	
10,9	0,2	0,1	CASHBIL	330		330				0,0	10,0 +	
12,0	8,4	4,0	CLICKS	660	670	670	670	670	10 +	1,5	13,5 –	8400V
9,8	10,2	4,1	CNAGALO			790				0,0	79,5 +	
4,8	21,0	6,7	CONTRAV		40	40	40	40		0,0	11,1 –	40

8.5 Events of DAYS +2 and +3: Wednesday 15 and Thursday 16 March 1989

Throughout Wednesday 15 March and Thursday 16 March the price of AUTOQUIP remains at 65 cents. However, the selling volume is drying up quickly, with only 20 775 shares traded on the former day, and the low figure of 6 000 on the latter.

8.6 Events of DAY +4: Friday 17 March 1989

By the close of trading on DAY +4 the share price has increased a further 5 cents to 70 cents. Only 17 600 shares changed hands.

Thus, from the appearance of its interim results on DAY 0, Monday 13 March 1989, up to DAY +4, Friday 17 March 1989, the AUTOQUIP share price has increased from 55 to 70 cents, *an absolutely magnificent increase of +27,3%*, and a total of 152 075 shares changed hands.

All this information is reflected in table 8.4.

AUTOQUIP featured as one of the top ten shares with regard to weekly price increase.

WEEKLY TOP 10 UP			
DALSIG	14	6+	75,0
AUTODEK	50	20+	66,7
OPECTRUM	65	20+	44,4
SWA FISH	1800	450+	33,3
AUTOQIP	70	15+	27,3
CARRIGS	50	10+	25,0
DBN DEEP	1500	300+	25,0
VCLEWIS	25	5+	25,0
MARKNOR	40	8+	25,0
EUREFIN	775	150+	24,0

8.7 Our AUTOQUIP shareholder has tasted blood

Our AUTOQUIP shareholder must surely spend a delightful weekend commencing Saturday 18 March 1989. After all, his shares have increased in price by 27,3% over the past week and he can look forward to Monday and, hopefully, continuation of this trend.

This is where he is to be proved oh so wrong.

Even after this 27,3% rise to 70 cents, according to table 8.4 the AUTOQUIP share is standing at a high dividend yield of 7,9% compared

Table 8.4 Events as at the close of Friday 17 March 1989. The AUTOQUIP share price has risen another 5 cents to a closing price of 70 cents, representing a magnificent increase of 27,3% in only one week. 152 075 shares are seen to have changed hands during this period

P.E.	E.Y.	D.Y.		BUY	SELL	LAST	H	L	D.M.	D.M.%	Y.M.%	D.V.	W.M.%	W.V.
						RETAILERS & WHOLSLRS								
4,6	21,6	5,9	AROMA		35	38S	38	38	2 –	5,0	45,7 –	6000V	11,6 –	17000
4,6	21,8	8,1	AKJ		50	50				0,0	25,0 +		0,0	5000
5,0	19,9	7,9	AUTOQIP	68	70	70	70	68	5 +	7,7	7,7 +	17600	27,3 +	152075
6,8	14,6	6,8	BERGERS		150	140				0,0	16,7 +		3,4 –	2500
12,4	8,1	3,2	BIDCORP	780		780	780	780	30 +	4,0	30,0 +	700	4,0 +	3600
		10,5	BIDCORP C	590		590			15 +	2,6	12,4 +		2,6 +	9000
5,0	20,0	6,8	BOYMANS	190		192				0,0	6,7 +		0,0	
10,9	9,2	3,1	CASHBIL	220		220				0,0	10,0 +		0,0	1600
12,5	8,0	3,9	*CLICKS	700		700	700	700	5 –	0,7	9,7 –	5400	7,7 +	63200
9,8	10,2	4,1	CNAGALO	790		790				0,0	79,5 +		0,0	5600
4,8	21,0	6,7	CONTRAV		40	40				0,0	11,1 –		5,3 +	360
5,4	18,6	8,6	CURNOW	35	40	35	38	35	3 –	7,9	30,0 –	27600V	2,8 –	68300
3,9	25,4	11,4	DECHOLD		50	50	50	50		0,0	9,1 –	3600	5,7 –	61000
3,7	27,3	12,7	DIALMOV			33	33	33		0,0	17,5 –	500	5,7 –	7000
3,1	32,3	12,3	DRIVTEC	65	66	65	65	63	2 +	3,2	23,5 –	14000	8,3 +	171792
6,7	15,0	9,0	DROPINN	38		40	40	40	2 +	5,3	0,0	85200V	14,3 +	109900
9,9	10,1	3,4	EDGARS	1775	1850	1750B				0,0	54,3 +		0,0	5200
		3,9	EDGARS CD	1775	2000	1667B				0,0	19,1 +		0,0	
7,7	13,0	4,5	FOCUS		50	50				0,0	25,0 +		0,0	45700
4,3	23,0	10,0	FLEIMAN	87	90	90	90	90		0,0	25,0 –	51000V	5,9 +	193800
9,9	10,1	4,2	FOSCHINI	4850		4850B				0,0	67,2 +		0,0	
4,6	21,5	5,2	FRASERS	800	700	575B				0,0,	36,1 –		0,0	1100
		16,1	FRASER CD	80		85				0,0	15,0 –		2,4 +	100
4,8	20,8	5,6	FRASCON	250	275	260				0,0	18,8 –		6,1 +	4000
			GARCON	SUS	PEN	DED								
5,4	18,4	7,4	GRESHAM	115	120	115	115	110	5 +	4,5	15,0 +	0000	1,2	82700
17,7	5,7	5,1	HISCORE	370	400	380	380	380	10 +	2,7	49,3 –	14750V	5,6 +	42337
4,1	24,2	7,8	HOMAKER	77	79	77	78	77	3 –	3,8	45,0 –	3395	0,0	148258
6,0	16,7	5,0	IBJOFFE		105	100				0,0	11,1 +		0,0	3000
2,8	35,9	5,3	*INTHOLD			625				0,0	13,6 +		0,0	
		8,9	INTH 7%CP			520				0,0	8,1 –		0,0	
		17,7	INTH 13CD			485				0,0	15,1 –		0,0	
5,1	19,5	7,6	JAZZ	75		75	75	72		0,0	60,0	14200V	10,3 +	35700
4,3	23,4	3,5	KIMET			100				0,0	42,9 +		0,0	7000
		11,1	KIMET 7%CP			85				0,0	15,0 –		0,0	
		21,7	KIMET 13CD			81				0,0	12,0 –		0,0	
11,1	9,0	3,8	LEFIC			2750				0,0	41,0 +		10,0 +	8700
10,6	9,4	4,7	MASCON		165	165				0,0	25,0 –		0,0	50
7,5	13,4	6,5	MASHOLD			170				0,0	12,8 –		0,0	1500
9,8	10,2	4,6	*METRO	485	495	490				0,0	21,6 –		0,0	272328
16,0	6,3	1,9	MIDAS	1300	1350	1350				0,0	145,5 +		3,1 +	650
5,2	19,4	7,1	MILSTAN	85		85	85	85		0,0	10,5 –	9100	6,3 +	46600
9,2	10,8	5,9	*O K	1600		1600	1600	1575	25 +	1,6	33,3 +	1500	4,6 +	8500
15,2	6,6	2,6	PENPIN		190	190				0,0	72,7 +		0,0	175
8,9	11,3	4,1	PEPGRO		1850	1800	1800	1800	50 –	2,7	5,9 +	800V	8,9 –	1368
		4,6	PEPGRO 7%			1500				0,0	58,9 +		0,0	
		6,2	PEPGRO 13		2050	1854				0,0	5,8 –		0,0	
8,9	11,2	3,8	*PEPKOR	3600	3700	3650	3650	3650		0,0	21,7 +	100	1,4 –	720
		5,2	PEPKOR 7%			2500				0,0	156,4 +		0,0	
		6,9	PEPKOR 13		3200	3044				0,0	22,1 +		0,0	
9,2	10,9	4,0	PEPSTOR		1350	1300				0,0	11,9 –		0,0	300
32,0	3,1	3,1	PIKWIK	550	600	550				0,0	44,7 +		3,5 –	22300
16,0	6,3	2,9	PICKNPAY	1200		1200	1200	1180	40 +	3,4	54,8 +	1200	2,1 +	49766
7,3	13,6	5,1	REGGIES	47	50	47	47	47	3 –	6,0	29,9 –	10150V	9,6 –	25558
4,7	21,3	9,5	SANLIC		40	40				0,0	20,0 –		0,0	8400
14,2	7,0	4,7	SCOCLIK	210	220	220	220	220		0,0	32,3 –	1880	0,0	110906
7,5	13,3	5,1	*SCORE	750	800	750	750	750		0,0	54,5 –	1300	6,3 –	4203
8,2	12,3	4,8	SHIELD	62	65	62	62	62		0,0	61,3 –	200	4,6	5800
13,2	7,6	3,2	SHOPRIT		275	270	270	270		0,0	8,0 +	3100V	0,0	4400
8,2	12,2	4,6	STORECO	840		840	840	840	10 +	1,2	24,4 +	3000V	1,8 +	8100
4,9	20,3	8,5	SPECTRUM	60	65	65	70	60	5 +	8,3	18,2 –	21715V	44,4 +	28840
3,8	26,2	6,3	SPITZ	165	180	175	175	175		0,0	75,0 +	1600V	0,0	1600
			SPITZ OPT			25				0,0	72,2 –		0,0	
3,6	28,1	10,0	SPRINGTEX		80	80				0,0	27,3 –		14,3 +	4800
5,2	19,2		*STERNS	170	175	170	170	170		0,0	13,3 +	200	0,0	200
4,5	22,0	7,2	TARRY	415	430	414B				0,0	3,5 +		0,0	
8,3	12,0	5,2	TELJOY	230		230	230	230		0,0	0,0	600	4,2 –	12700
10,2	9,8		TRABILD	50		55	55	50	5 +	10,0	83,3 +	13400V	0,0	13650
		13,9	TRABILD P			61				0,0	18,7 –		0,0	
			TRABILD C			53				0,0	6,0 +		0,0	
2,8	36,2	5,1	*TRADGRO	175		175	175	170	5 +	2,9	16,7 +	48100V	2,9 +	78760
		13,7	TRADGR PP		95	95				0,0	0,0		5,0 +	2000
		16,3	TRADGR CP	195		210	210	210		0,0	5,0 +	10700V	0,0	40700
		9,5	TRGR A7CP	110		110	110	110		0,0	8,3 –	397V	0,0	515
		10,8	TRGR 13CD	175	185	180				0,0	20,0 +		0,0	
		10,3	TRGR 130CD	175	200	190				0,0	8,6 +		6,0	25000
4,6	21,9	9,3	VADEK		43	43				0,0	21,8 –		0,0	11200
12,5	8,0	2,7	WALHOLD	550	590	550	550	550	20 +	3,8	66,7 +	2800	4,8 +	7200
12,4	8,1	2,7	*WALTONS	560	570	565	565	555	10 +	1,8	63,8 +	9300	2,7 +	77338
10,5	9,5	4,0	*WOOLTRU	2250		2300				0,0	73,6 +		2,3 –	6812
10,5	9,5	4,0	*WOOLTRU-A	2250		2300	2300	2300		0,0	80,4 +	13200V	2,3 –	20500
	8,3	4,9	AVERAGE DAYS TRADE TOTALS						R**866552			VOL		407287

with the sector average of 4,9%, and its earning yield is the high figure of 19,9% compared with the sector average of 8,3%. It would appear that the share still has a good rise ahead of it before it attains anything approaching the sector average dividend or earnings yield figures.

Why, then, do I state that our shareholder is now incorrect in expecting the previous week's rise in price to continue? I have stated often in this text that my aim is an increase of 40% in the share price over the period of one year. Yet here with AUTOQUIP we have had an increase of 27,3% in only one week.

The experienced buyer of these shares will now step back and take a cool bird's-eye view of events. The only way in which the share price will rise further is through enthusiasm on the part of prospective buyers. The latter have seen what can only be described as an extremely sharp price increase over the past week, and now wish to cool matters somewhat.

This topic of 'cooling matters' after a sharp price rise in a share is of such importance that it is dealt with in considerable detail in chapter 9. In the meantime, I point out only some of the factors of which the reader should be aware.

First, at any one time only the minority of shareholders will have accurate knowledge of the true value of the shares they possess. Any experienced participant in the Stock Exchange will agree with me on this issue. For many years now it has been my contention that if this were not so, most of the absolutely foolhardy price increases that occur during the mad stampede of a typical bull market phase just could not occur. Similarly, if the average shareholder was aware of the true value of his shares, most of the unduly sharp price falls that occur just after the crash of our previously mentioned bull market would not take place. Hence my opinion, based on detailed observation over many years, that the average shareholder is really ignorant of the true value of his shares.

In the case of a sharp price rise, as has taken place with AUTOQUIP, sellers are prone to appear once it is apparent that the steam has gone out of what can only be termed buyer enthusiasm for the share. These sellers wish to take their profits and disappear from the AUTOQUIP scene.

What is actually happening with regard to the supposed lack of enthusiasm on the part of prospective AUTOQUIP buyers *is exactly the opposite* of what the sellers assume. It is precisely because of their enthusiasm that these buyers are prepared to wait on the sidelines for the sellers to appear.

Our mature AUTOQUIP shareholder has to acquire the highly desirable character trait known as patience. Knowing that his aim is only a 40% price rise in one year, he must be prepared to sit back and retain his shares without the weekly expectation of any further increase in share price.

In other words, to his previously acquired highly desirable character trait of confidence, our Stock Exchange investor is to add patience. It is my opinion that, particularly at a time when a share price has increased at what can only be described as an unduly fast pace, patience is far and away the more difficult to aspire to.

It is possibly the feeling of an anticlimax that makes the acquisition of patience so difficult. For some three weeks now our AUTOQUIP shareholder has seen his shares begin to rise, albeit at a slow pace initially, then accelerate, and finally go full steam ahead to a 27% increase in only one week. He has tasted blood – this is possibly the simplest manner of describing our shareholder's attitude to his investment – and he wishes to taste more of the same, please!

To be told at this blood-tasting stage that it is *because* of this blood that he must expect to have no more, is an exceedingly difficult and disappointing experience for our shareholder. The easiest way of convincing him that this is what is required is by re-emphasising the aim of a 40% share price increase *over the period of a full year*. He has achieved by far the greater portion of this goal in a short period; therefore now he must sit back and relax.

At this stage our shareholder will inevitably ask a question such as: 'For how long am I expected to sit back and relax?', and he will not be particularly pleased with the answer: *For the period of six months until the next set of financial results appear*. In fact, in my experience he will be completely devastated by this answer. Having had the delightful experience of a 27% rise in one week, how can he possibly sit back and kick his heels? The feeling of anticlimax is just too much to bear.

Over and over, this type of investor will repeat his view that even after its sharp rise, AUTOQUIP is still apparently completely undervalued compared with the sector averages. Its dividend yield is still, as I indicated earlier, 7,9% compared with the sector average of only 4,9%, and its earnings yield is the high figure of 19,9% compared with the sector average of 8,3%. Our inexperienced investor is convinced that I am wrong and that the share price must rise.

He has overlooked, of course, the most fundamental of all questions concerning Stock Exchange operations. This is: **What makes the price of a share rise?**

This is of such import that the whole of chapter 9 is devoted to answering it.

9

There is no body of wise men allocating prices to shares

Page

9.1 Introduction

Many inexperienced Stock Exchange participants seem to imagine that there is a body of wise men with white hair and long flowing beards which meets daily, presumably on the top floor of the Exchange building, to decide on the price of each share featuring on the boards of the Johannesburg Stock Exchange. It would appear that a member of this group of sages merely points a finger at, say AUTOQUIP, and states that in view of its interim results, the price of 70 cents will be allocated to it. I have conjured up this picturesque scene after years of hearing this question from impatient shareholders: 'Why hasn't my share moved?'

If only such a committee of sages could be appointed, all the troubles conventionally associated with Stock Exchange investment would disappear. However, in the absence thereof, it must be remembered that all dealings on the Stock Exchange are of a supply and demand nature.

This simple phrase 'of a supply and demand nature' contains a multitude of complexities. The aim of this chapter is to reveal some of these.

9.2 Only one occurrence causes a share price to rise

Often a share price remains constant during the day of, and during subsequent days after, the appearance of what seems to be a magnificent set of financial results. In such cases I am often telephoned with the inevitable question: 'But why hasn't my share moved?'

This type of shareholder seems to think that the committee of sages has met and forgotten to consider the share in question. It can be extremely difficult to convince such an investor that *only one occurrence causes a share price to increase.*

A buyer enthusiastic enough to offer a price greater than the ruling share price must appear on the scene.

The really devastating aspect of this information is that *the shareholder himself is completely incapable of setting the ball in motion*, unless of course he himself wishes to assume the role of a buyer and thereby raise the share price.

Thus, no matter how convinced or enthusiastic a shareholder may be about the undervalued qualities of his share, *unless and until another investor is of the same opinion, the share price will not move.*

I am often asked how the spreading of information about the desirability of a certain share can be achieved. Tongue in cheek, but often more seriously, I have replied that a shareholder should stand in front of the Stock Exchange building holding a board stating in large letters: BUY XY SHARES. THEY ARE UNDERVALUED! I see no reason why this manoeuvre should not be adopted. It would most certainly have the desired effect of bringing to the attention of those who have missed this situation the extent of their omission.

In the absence of such board-waving, the conventional manner of spreading information about shares worthy of purchase takes four avenues. Each of these is discussed below.

9.3 Disseminating share selections: the role of the daily financial press

The daily financial press plays a vital role in disseminating information concerning shares listed on the Johannesburg Stock Exchange. This role can be divided into two functions; first, *publishing* the latest financial results of a listed company, and second, *commenting on* the standard of these results and offering some *analysis* of the company concerned.

Without his daily financial newspaper, the Stock Exchange participant would receive his ardently awaited information about the most recent company financial results far too late to take the correct action. Thus the as-soon-as-received publication of company financial statements is a *sine qua non* for the investor.

I still stand by my initial opinion that by far the majority of Stock Exchange participants are not in a position to analyse these financial results for themselves and hence have to rely on the analyses of others. Conventionally, simultaneously with the publication of a set of company results in the daily financial press, there will appear a commentary and an analysis of the standard of the emergent figures.

Unfortunately, due to space restrictions or other obvious reasons, this analysis is inevitably on the brief side. However, with this book beside him, the Stock Exchange participant should be in a position to analyse the financial results in the required detail for himself.

9.4 Weekly financial magazines

The conventional weekly financial magazine appears on a Thursday and devotes space to those companies whose annual reports have recently been published. This analysis is detailed, but really too late to allow the Stock Exchange investor as I envisage him to take the required action.

However, the appearance of a listed company in such a magazine invariably sparks off some action in the share. If the comment is favourable, buying action will become evident immediately.

9.5 The Sunday financial press

There is something about the Sunday financial press which carries great weight with conventional Stock Exchange participants. Possibly it has something to do with the fact that on a Sunday they are relaxed and away from the busy office routine, and thus are able to read the comments expressed and digest them fully at their leisure.

Such comments are normally restricted to an in-depth analysis of one or two companies whose performance on the Stock Exchange boards has been unnecessarily slow. In other words, despite the high standards of the financial results already achieved, the share price has barely moved. The analysis is conventionally of an extremely high standard, and the detail shown is always appreciated by the investor.

A share thus recommended by the normal Sunday financial newspaper will show immediate response on the following Monday. I have found this to occur without fail, depending of course on the standard of the recommendation made. The phrase 'due to favourable weekend press comment' will often be found in commentaries in the daily financial press on undue and profound increases in activity in previously languishing shares.

Be that as it may, I have found such knowledgeable and detailed weekend financial commentary an excellent manner of causing intense interest in a share whose price has remained dormant for reasons which can only be described as unjustified.

An investor who some days or weeks previously purchased such a share, that is immediately upon the publication of its financial results, and sees this share favourably analysed and recommended in the Sunday press, can sit back and relax. That share will invariably cease to be dormant and move in the desired direction.

9.6 Stockbrokers' research departments

Stockbrokers' research departments publish weekly newsletters in which the merits of various shares are analysed. The circulation of such newsletters is restricted to the clients of the stockbroker concerned, and is thus much lower than that of the financial press.

Nevertheless, what it lacks in quantity such a stockbroker investment newsletter makes up for in quality. A client who receives this document is usually sufficiently well-endowed that his buying order will be for a relatively large quantity of the share or shares recommended.

Sudden buying activity in a share can often be traced to a favourable recommendation in one or more investment newsletters emanating from the research departments of stockbrokers.

9.7 The attitude of mind required of the correct Stock Exchange investor

The correct Stock Exchange investor is one who obeys implicitly all of my nine laws, as given in chapter 3. Once he has selected and purchased his shares on this basis, I merely ask him to be patient if the price increase that he was anticipating does not materialise immediately.

Rarely will a share chosen on the basis of these nine laws not move at all. I have yet to find such a share which does not increase in price within the first week of the publication of a set of favourable financial results.

However, the price increase may not satisfy the expectations of some investors. Of course in many instances these expectations may be unreasonable, but to the correct investor whose demands are not excessive and whose shares have barely moved in price I say with experience: '*Just be patient and wait*'.

At some stage, not necessarily in the next two to three weeks, his well-chosen share will be selected for detailed analysis and comment by one of the financial media indicated earlier. I speak from experience when I say that this just has to happen. When it does, the investor can sit back as his confidence in his investment abilities is restored or reinforced.

Therefore I reiterate that the first desirable character trait for a successful campaign of Stock Exchange investment is *confidence*. The second and often more difficult to acquire desirable character trait is *patience*.

With a suitable combination of these two traits, the correctly operating Stock Exchange investor will inevitably succeed in his goals.

9.8 The share price rises only in response to favourable information

Section 9.7 was concerned specifically with the type of share whose standard of financial results is exemplary, in that it obeys the relevant seven laws, but whose price languished after their publication.

At this stage the situation will be discussed which occurred with the interim results of AUTOQUIP, shown in the previous chapter, where there is an immediate and large rise in share price upon the appearance of the financial results, but thereafter the price remains constant for many months. In point of fact, the price remains constant until the appearance of the next set of results, six months later.

The most important point for the correctly operating Stock Exchange investor to realise in this regard is that *fundamentally a share price will rise only in response to favourable information*. In the normal run of events, *this latter favourable information becomes available only twice a year*, first when the interim results are published, and second, when the preliminary results are published. It must be appreciated that the time interval between these two occurrences is then a full six months.

Fundamentally, therefore, *an investor must be prepared for action in the share price on only two occasions during the financial year*. Once he has come to grips with this information, it is possible that his initial feelings of impatience upon seeing his share price stay constant month after month may disappear.

Once again I remind him of my fundamental goal for an increase in share price. This is the magnitude of 40% over the period of one full year. All that I want is an initial 20% rise in share price after the appearance of the interim results, and a further 20% rise six months later upon the appearance of the preliminary results. If this is achieved, I am completely happy for the share price to remain dormant inbetween time.

9.9 The possibility of a price rise between the final and interim results

Above I emphasised the fundamental consideration pertaining to the much awaited occurrence of a rise in the investor's share price. This is that it will occur only in response to favourable information about the share.

In the six months just after the appearance of the interim financial results, there is really nothing which normally will yield such a desirable piece of information. In the six months after the appearance of the *final* results, on the other hand, there are two occurrences which may well afford the information required.

The first of these is *the appearance of the company's annual report.* Conventionally this occurs approximately one month after the publication of the preliminary results. The report contains the Chairman's Review of the company's past activities, and, more important now to the investor, his prognostications of the company's prospects for the forthcoming year.

In such prognostications we find three distinct degrees of optimism on the part of the Chairman concerned. The remark that it is hoped that the company's *pre-tax* profits for the forthcoming financial year will at least equal those of the previous year is the lowest degree of optimism. The next degree of optimism is that the company's earnings-per-share, which are recognised as involving the *after-tax* profits, should be at least equal to those of the previous year. The third, and most optimistic prognostication, will take the following form: 'despite anticipations of a slowdown in the economy, we look forward to a substantial increase in earnings-per-share in the new year'.

The appearance of this last statement in a company's annual report is virtually guaranteed to result in an increase in the share price. Buyers become extremely enthusiastic about the share concerned and hence are likely to cause a price rise in their efforts to acquire the share. After the release of a set of favourable preliminary financial results, nothing is more conducive to a substantial price rise in the share than the appearance of a Chairman's optimistic prognostication of prospects for the year ahead.

The above discussion concerns the role the appearance of a favourable annual report can play in causing a price increase in a share. There is a second factor which may give a push to the share price. This is the annual general meeting of the company.

The annual general meeting, or AGM as it is more commonly known, can affect the share price favourably. Normally it takes place one month after the release of the company's annual report, and hence the contents of the latter form by far the greater portion of the AGM proceedings. Some prospective share buyers are not content merely to read of the company's prospects in the forthcoming year, they actually need to question the Chairman in some detail in this regard as well. If such questions are answered to the satisfaction of all concerned, once again a share price rise will conventionally occur.

As shown above, the company's annual report appears one month after the release of the preliminary results and the AGM one month later. In the first six months of the financial year, therefore, in the normal run of events a price rise in the share is experienced in three distinct stages: the first, upon the appearance of the prelims; the second, upon the appearance of the annual report; and the third upon the staging of the AGM. For the four months which remain until the appearance of the next set of financial results, the new interims, the shareholder must be prepared for no action at all in his share price. This may appear something of an anti-climax to him, since this new dormancy in price occurs just after some often 'blood-tasting' increases. My only comment now is that patience must be exercised.

I regard the possibility of price rises in a share on more than two occasions during the financial year as a welcome bonus, and not as the norm. I am completely satisfied with what can be called a 'two-step' rise in the price of my shares – one after the appearance of the interim results and the other after the appearance of the preliminary results. However, the sum of these two steps must total 40% or more to obtain my complete approval.

9.10 Choosing additional shares to have staggered year ends

It has been seen that there is a high degree of probability of zero activity in a share price for the six month period between the appearance of the interim and preliminary results in the first place, and for the four month period between the holding of the company's AGM and the appearance of the new interim results in the second. There may be some investors whose patience, no matter what soothing noises I make in this regard, is severely tested by these long periods of share price dormancy.

There is a simple solution for this type of investor. This is to purchase shares in companies *whose financial year ends are nine months staggered from their existing shares*. For example, in the case of AUTOQUIP, with its June 30 financial year end, additional shares could be purchased in a company with a March 30 year end. Let us call our shares in this latter company share Y: we now have the following financial calendar:

June 30	AUTOQUIP year end – preliminary results soon to appear
Sept 30	Y interim results soon to appear
Dec 31	AUTOQUIP interims soon to appear
Mar 31	Y financial year end – preliminary results soon to appear

Thus the dreaded six months of inactivity after the appearance of the interim results is avoided, as is the four months of dormancy after the AGM in each case.

9.11 The prime causes of a severe drop in a share price

I have devoted ten sections in this chapter to discussing the topic of a rise in share price. I now come to the opposite end of the scale and consider the occurrence of a sharp drop in price and its causes.

In contrast to a rise in price, a drop in price can be dismissed very succinctly, as follows. Ignoring shareholders who sell their shares in order to meet recent financial commitments, since such action will not normally affect the share price dramatically, there are really only two reasons for a sharp decline in the price of a share.

The first and most common reason is a thorough and well-founded feeling of disillusion on the part of a large number of shareholders in a recently released set of financial results by the company concerned. The disenchantment felt by such shareholders who were expecting good results sets into action wave upon wave of heavy selling of the share, and its price falls dramatically in a very short period. I will consider the specific example of the share MIDAS in chapter 11, where a 50% drop in price occurred in only two months. Thus all further discussion of this reason is reserved for chapter 11.

The second reason is a feeling of trepidation on the part of shareholders. This occurs most often with what are termed 'blue chip' shares, where, as will be discussed in detail in chapter 12, the share price has risen way beyond all logical appraisal of its true value. We may draw analogy of a house of cards in such a situation – any slight breath of wind is capable of affecting these cards dramatically. Such a breath can originate in events as far afield as America or Japan, and when viewed quite coolly and dispassionately should not really affect our share market in the manner that they conventionally do. However, more on this score in later chapters.

9.12 Conclusion

The severe implications of the Stock Exchange being a supply and demand based sphere of operations are illustrated in detail in this chapter. Two attitudes of mind on the part of investors are seen to predominate here. The first is a feeling of justified confidence on the part of the knowledgeable shareholder, which is based on accurate quantitative appraisal of relevant financial results. The second is a feeling of fear, and here we have confirmation of the saying that conventionally fear is based on ignorance.

The vagaries of a supply and demand situation are great indeed on these grounds.

10

AUTOQUIP's final results for the year ended 30 June 1989

Page

10.1 Introduction

Chapter 3 discusses in great detail the financial results achieved by AUTOQUIP in the six month period ended 31 December 1988, in other words its *interim* results. This chapter analyses AUTOQUIP's results for the full financial year ended 30 June 1989, that is its *final* results. Once again I will do this on the basis of a detailed consideration of the original release as it appeared in the financial press.

The relevant release, shown in figure 10.1, appeared in the morning press on 19 September 1989.

10.2 Detailed analysis of figure 10.1

A really thorough analysis of the interim results having been given in chapter 3, there is no need to repeat the details of the principles involved. Hence I will proceed rapidly with a step-by-step evaluation of AUTOQUIP's year end financial results as depicted in figure 10.1.

- ☐ Step 1 The year-on-year increase in our prime quantity of the earnings-per-share (eps) is seen to be the magnificent figure of 50%. The previous eps was 10,5 cents. It has now risen to 15,7 cents. Thus the first hurdle has been jumped in fine fashion.

Figure 10.1

AUTOQUIP GROUP·LIMITED

(Registration No 87/02838/06)
Incorporated in the Republic of South Africa

Directors: GJ Santana (Chairman), BD Coquelle (Managing director), GR Coombes, CS Seabrooke

Audited results and declaration of dividend for the year ended 30 June 1989

OPERATING INCOME UP 101% • GROUP EARNINGS UP 66%

Financial results
The consolidated audited results are as follows:

Consolidated income statement

	1989 R000s	1988 R000s	% change
Turnover	**35 546**	22 163	+ 60
Operating income	**5 205**	2 588	+ 101
Finance charges	**583**	175	
Net income before taxation	**4 622**	2 413	+ 92
Taxation	**2 161**	904	
Net income after taxation	**2 461**	1 509	+ 63
Share of income – foreign operations	**53**	–	
	2 514	1 509	
Minority shareholders	**3**	–	
Net income attributable to shareholders	**2 511**	1 509	+ 66
Weighted average number of shares in issue (000's)	**16 000**	14 400	+ 11
Earnings per share (cents)	15,7	10,5	+ 50
Dividends per share (cents)	**6,5**	3,0*	+ 44
*(1988 annualised 4,5 cents)			
Dividend cover	**2,4**	2,3*	

Consolidated balance sheet

	1989 R000s	1988 R000s
Capital employed		
Stated capital	**4 857**	4 857
Distributable reserve	**2 500**	1 029
Shareholders funds	**7 357**	5 886
Medium term liabilities	**350**	146
Minority shareholders	**3**	–
	7 710	6 032
Employment of capital		
Fixed assets and investments	**1 174**	1 200
Net current assets	**6 536**	4 832
Current assets	**19 648**	12 177
Current liabilities	**13 112**	7 345
	7 710	6 032
Net tangible asset value per share	**46 cents**	36,8 cents

Comments

Profile
The Autoquip division is a wholesaler and retailer of exclusive automotive accessories and performance tyres. The Partquip division is a specialist wholesaler of selective automotive parts whilst the Techniquip division is a distributor of industrial bearings and allied products.

Results
The group is again proud to announce significant increases in turnover, operating income and earnings for the financial year ending June 1989. The group's growth has been organic and is as a result of increased market share in all divisions. Over this period the considerable emphasis placed on the sourcing of products together with rigorous financial controls has resulted in an overall increase in margins. A centralised administration infrastructure combined with an upgraded computer system linking all operations has also increased efficiency and produced cost savings.

Foreign operations
The contribution to the group's profitability by our foreign operation is very encouraging particularly in view of the fact that full account has been taken of all startup costs.

New developments
During this financial year the Techniquip division expanded its operations to Natal utilising the existing regional warehouse and administration infrastructure in Durban.

In March a new branch of the Autoquip division was opened in Vanderbijlpark positioned so as to take full advantage of the Vaal Triangle market.

A new division of Partquip has been established. Trading as Partco, this division will continue with the group's philosophy of niche marketing and will specialise in the sourcing and distribution of steering, suspension and rubber components.

Prospects
A new branch will be opened in Port Elizabeth during October to service the Eastern Cape and will be structured so as to accommodate all divisions. This branch will enable the group to increase its market share in this area and will make a contribution to the group's profitability in the 1990 financial year.

The board is confident that with the ageing vehicle population and spiralling new vehicle prices all automotive divisions within the group are ideally positioned to capitalise on the growing parts and accessory market and we forecast real growth in earnings for the 1990 financial year.

Dividends
A final dividend of 4,0 cents per share has been declared making a total of 6,5 cents for the year. The dividend will be paid to shareholders registered on Friday, 29 September 1989 and will be paid on or about 16 October 1989.

BD Coquelle *Managing director*
GR Coombes *Director*

18 September 1989

Registered office
6th Floor
Saambou National Building
130 Commissioner Street
Johannesburg, 2001

Transfer secretaries
Fraser Street Registrars
(Pty) Limited
Ground Floor
65 President Street
Johannesburg, 2001

☐ Step 2 The dividends per share have increased by 44% to 6,5 cents. More could not have been asked on this score.

☐ Step 3 The performance of AUTOQUIP is actually better than that indicated in steps 1 and 2, since the average number of shares in issue has increased by 11% during the year, that is from 14,4 million to 16 million. The actual net income attributable to shareholders increased by a magnificent 66%.

☐ Step 4 Now for the first look at the balance sheet, the item of prime importance here being medium-term liabilities. We note an increase from R0,146 million to R0,35 million, and our eyebrows lift slightly on this score. However, in terms of my sixth law events are still satisfactory, since the ratio of medium-term liabilities to shareholders' funds is only 0,35/7,357 or 4,78%, which is well below my maximum allowable of 20%. However, this ratio is greater than the 2,48% of the previous year end. We must watch carefully for the consequence hereof.

☐ Step 5 This consequence is seen to be a finance charge of R0,583 million compared with the previous figure of only R0,175 million. In terms of ratios, finance charges are now 11,2% of the operating income of R5,505 million, compared with the previous 6,76% of the previous operating income of R2,588 million. However this situation is completely acceptable, since net income before taxation has increased by the more than acceptable figure of 92%. However, we will watch these medium-term liabilities in future financial reports.

☐ Step 6 Taxation, at R2,161 million, is now at the rate of 46,75% compared with the far lower rate of 37,46% pertaining in the previous financial year. Thus our 92% increase in pre-tax income is reduced to a 63% after-tax increase.

☐ Step 7 The return on capital employed, in terms of my seventh law, is the figure of the pre-tax R4,622 million divided by the capital employed of R7,71 million, or 59,95%. This represents what can only be described as a magnificent achievement, since the figure for the previous year was 2,413/6,032, or only 40%.

☐ Step 8 The directors' comments must now be appraised. Personally I could not ask for a more positive attitude, particularly when I read the final summary:

> The board is confident that with the ageing vehicle population and spiralling new vehicle prices all automotive divisions within the group are ideally positioned to capitalise on the growing parts and accessory market, and we forecast real growth in earnings for the 1990 financial year.

10.3 The smile on the shareholder's face

The smile now appearing on the shareholder's face is worthy of a photograph! All that I wrote in chapter 3 concerning the ability to select a company of adequate financial pedigree has apparently come to fruition. A better set of financial results could not have been asked for.

AUTOQUIP's share price rose from 72 cents just prior to the release of the information contained in figure 10.1 to 87 cents two weeks later. I will not detail the daily volume of sales here, as I did in chapter 8, since the enthusiastic reader is in a position to obtain these for himself, should he deem it necessary.

This 20,8% rise in share price in a matter of a fortnight may coolly be appraised as 'adequate or quite satisfactory'! On a price of 87 cents, however, AUTOQUIP was still standing on a dividend yield of a high 6,5/87, or 7,5%, compared with the sector average of some 5% at that time. Thus it should still have been regarded as an underpriced share at this new 87 cents.

Then, just as AUTOQUIP was poised for a further and merited increase in share price, along came an equivalent company with a disturbing set of financial results. I use the word 'equivalent' here to indicate a company operating in the same field as AUTOQUIP, namely automotive spares and accessories. This was the company called MIDAS, which previously was quite the glamour share of this industry.

MIDAS' balance sheet and income statement are analysed in detail in chapter 11 and the panic situation which arose in a short time among certain share analysts concerning the previously highly regarded automotive spares industry is appraised in considerable detail.

Completely unjustifiably, in my opinion, AUTOQUIP was to be caught up in the wake of MIDAS' unsatisfactory results and thus to suffer a heavy setback. More about this in chapter 11.

11

Beware the company which transgresses my sixth law concerning the ratio of medium-term liabilities to shareholders' funds

11.1 Introduction

Some reviewers of my first book, *Winning on the JSE*, have expressed the opinion that my laws regarding the required financial pedigree of a company are too stringent. In particular Laws 6 and 7, dealing respectively with the ratio of medium-term liabilities to shareholders' funds and the return on capital employed, have been singled out for comment.

In this chapter I deal with a company called MIDAS, which for some years was the darling of the Stock Exchange community but which suddenly, in November 1989, lost all its popularity and halved its share price in only two months.

As will be shown here, a severe violation of Law 6 took place and the poor performance which arose thereafter was, in my opinion, to be expected. It was extremely unfortunate that share analysts quite illogically tarred AUTOQUIP with the same brush and that it suffered, if only for a short while, a fate similar to that of MIDAS.

11.2 MIDAS' track record

MIDAS is a company operating in the same sphere as AUTOQUIP. It was first listed on the JSE in 1986 and its earnings-per-share and dividend declarations were as shown below for the financial year end 28 February in each case.

	1987	*1988*	*1989*
Earnings-per-share (cents)	34,7	61,2	118,8
Dividend per share (cents)	11	20	35
Highest share price reached (cents)	430	810	1400

This is indeed a most impressive track record. The share's popularity among the investment community can be imagined, with the fantastic percentage increases indicated year-on-year in both earnings-per-share and dividends.

However as always, in my opinion, such popularity is overdone. The price of the share is always overvalued as far as I am concerned. In confirmation of this look at table 8.4, which depicts events at the close on Friday 17 March 1989. This was the week after the release of AUTOQUIP's interim results.

MIDAS also falls under the section RETAILERS AND WHOLESALERS on the Stock Exchange page. We note that its closing price was 1350 cents, offering a dividend yield of the ridiculously low figure of 1,9% and a price earnings ratio of the high figure of 16. As can be seen, the sector average on that date was a dividend yield of 4,9% and a price earnings ratio of 12. To me, no matter what its previous track record, MIDAS had to be regarded as an overvalued share on these figures. I was even more convinced on this score when its final results for the year ended 28 February 1989 appeared in the financial press on the 29 April. This is the subject of the following section.

11.3 MIDAS' final results for the year ended 28 February 1989

MIDAS' results as released in the financial press appear in figure 11.1. In my analysis of these figures I will adopt the same sequence of eight steps used for AUTOQUIP in chapter 10.

☐ Step 1 The year-on-year increase in earnings-per-share is seen to be the really outstanding figure of 94%, that is up from 61,2 cents to an overwhelming 118,8 cents.

☐ Step 2 The dividend increase is the superb figure of 75%, that is up from 20 cents to 35 cents.

☐ Step 3 The number of shares in issue increased by 8% to 13,155 million. The profit attributable to shareholders thus increased by the extraordinary figure of 110%. What more, stated many share analysts, could one possibly ask of a company?

☐ Step 4 Now for the prime item of medium-term liabilities in the balance sheet. *Here comes the first black mark. These have increased nearly five times*, that is from R4,122 million to R19,616 million. Among the knowledgeable, eyebrows should be raised far more than slightly on this score. In point of fact, eyebrows might well hit the ceiling, if this were physically possible!

I make this remark because the ratio of interest-bearing debt to shareholders' funds is now the alarming figure of 19,616/46,914, or 41,8%. In the previous year it was only 4,122/33,972, or 12,1%.

Law 6 does not permit a figure over 20% for this all-important ratio. In my mind, at any rate, *alarm bells begin to ring*.

☐ Step 5 The vital consequence of Step 4 is that the interest paid has jumped from R0,537 million in the previous year to the staggering figure of R2,268 million in the year under review.

Figure 11.1

MIDAS LIMITED

(Registration No. 68/02260/06
(Incorporated in the Republic of South Africa)

AUDITED YEAR END RESULTS AND DIVIDEND ANNOUNCEMENT

★ **Turnover up 84%**

★ **Earnings per share up 94%**

★ **Dividends up 75%**

★ **Increased earnings forecast**

The audited results for the twelve months ended 28 February 1989, compared with the same period the previous year, are as follows:

CONSOLIDATED INCOME STATEMENT	**Year ended February**		
	1989	**1988**	**Change**
	R'000	**R'000**	**%**
Turnover	**175 949**	95 420	+84
Operating profit	**20 866**	9 698	+115
Interest paid	**2 268**	537	+322
Profit before taxation	**18 598**	9 161	+103
Taxation	**3 336**	2 496	+34
Profit after taxation	**15 262**	6 665	+129
Dividends received	–	65	-
Income of the group	**15 262**	6 730	+127
Attributable income of associates	**370**	706	-48
Profit attributable to shareholders before extraordinary items	**15 632**	7 436	+110
Extraordinary items	**3 500**	229	+1 428
Profit attributable to shareholders	**12 132**	7 207	+68
Number of ordinary shares in issue	**13 154 715**	12 143 190	+8
Earnings per share (cents)	**118,8**	61,2	+94
Interim dividend (cents)	**14,0**	8,0	+75
Final dividend (cents)	**21,0**	12,0	+75
Total dividend (cents)	**35,0**	20,0	+75
Dividend cover (times)	**3,4**	3,1	

CONSOLIDATED BALANCE SHEET			
Shareholders interest	**46 914**	33 972	+38
Interest bearing debt	**19 616**	4 122	+376
Interest-free liabilities	**28 001**	21 283	+32
Total Capital Employed	**94 531**	59 377	+59
Fixed assets	**6 116**	4 701	+30
Investments	**16 753**	9 433	+78
Current assets	**71 662**	45 243	+58
Total Assets	**94 531**	59 377	+59
Shareholders interest to total assets	**49,6%**	57,2%	
Gearing	**41,8%**	12,1%	

Financial

The group's performance during the financial year under review exceeded expectations. Turnover increased by 84% to R176-million. This growth was achieved as a consequence of substantial organic expansion together with the acquisition of the Akals and Champion Motor Supplies businesses.

Earnings per share increased by 94% to 118,8 cents while operating margins rose from 10,2% to 11,9% when compared with the previous year. The higher margins are as a consequence of changes in the product mix and the absence of certian non-recurring costs. The group's balance sheet remains sound. Management consciously decided to increase stock because of anticipated higher demand.

Goodwill of R3 500 000 has been written off in terms of the group's accounting policy. Furthermore, an amount of R682 000 has been written off against trading profits in order to provide for enhanced pension fund benefits.

Prospects

The favourable factors which influenced the past year's results still persist and as a consequence earnings per share for the financial year ending February 1990 are expected to be higher than those currently reported.

Declaration of Dividend No 27

Notice is hereby given that on 28 April 1989, the directors declared a final dividend of 21,0 cents per share to shareholders registered in the books of the company at the close of business on 19 May 1989. The transfer register of the company will be closed from 20 May 1989 to 27 May 1989, both days inclusive. Shareholders are advised that any change in address and or dividend instructions must be lodged with the Transfer Secretaries on or before 19 May 1989. Non-resident shareholders' tax will be deducted where applicable. Dividend cheques will be posted on 2 June 1989.

By order of the Board

DB Riley – Chairman
GL von Loeper – Chief Executive Officer

Directors
DB Riley (Chairman)
GL von Loeper (Managing)
WC Akal
WP Benz
SJ de Vos
RD Gudegast
BC McCarthy
L Miller
D Saville
GM Walker

Registered Office
9 Old Main Pretoria Road
Halfway House
Midrand, 1685

Transfer Secretaries
Central Registrars Limited
154 Market Street
Johannesburg, 2001
PO Box 4844
Johannesburg, 2000

☐ Step 6 The taxation rate has dropped significantly. It is now only 17,9% compared with the previously pertaining 27,2%. This will ameliorate the situation regarding the increased interest charges.

☐ Step 7 The return on capital employed is now 18,598/94,531, or 19,7%, compared with the previous 9,161/59,377, or 15,4%. Thus there has been an improvement on this score, although the figure of 19,7% is lower than what is wished for.

☐ Step 8 The directors are still optimistic, commenting:

> The favourable factors which influenced the past year's results still persist and as a consequence earnings-per-share for the financial year ending February 1990 are expected to be higher than those currently reported.

On this basis the share price kept rising to a maximum of 1450 cents.

11.4 MIDAS' interim results for the period ended 31 August 1989

Some readers may consider me an undue pessimist. With absolutely fantastic increases in earnings-per-share and dividends, what more could I possibly ask for? My answer is, of course, a far lower ratio of long-term loans to shareholders' funds than the 41,8% pertaining. This violates my Law 6 and to me is not an acceptable situation.

Now to analyse MIDAS' results released six months after those in figure 11.1. Figure 11.2 shows the interim results for the priod ended 31 August 1989, which appeared in the financial press on 4 October 1989.

To our horror, the increase in earnings-per-share is the insignificant figure of 5,3%, with a mere 3,6% increase in the interim dividend. In the light of the previous 'whopping' increases in these quantities, we must take a close look at the cause of this great diminution in performance.

We come across it immediately in the item 'interest paid'. To our consternation we see that the interest paid of R2,06 million for the six month period under analysis is nearly the same as the R2,268 million

Figure 11.2

MIDAS LIMITED

(Registration No. 68/02260/06
(Incorporated in the Republic of South Africa)

INTERIM REPORT TO SHAREHOLDERS

Group Profit
The consolidated profit, unaudited, for the half year ended 31 August 1989 compared with the same period of the previous year and for the year ended February 1989, is as follows:

Consolidated Income Statement

	Half year ended August 1989 R'000	Half year ended Agugust 1988 R'000	Change %	Year ended February 1989 R'000
Turnover	93 683	78 055	+20,0	175 949
Operating profit	10 809	8 508	+27,1	20 866
Interest paid	2 060	362	+469,1	2 268
Profit before taxation	8 749	8 146	+7,4	18 598
Taxation	1 616	1 621	–	3 336
Profit after taxation	7 133	6 525	+9,3	15 262
Attributable income of associates	44	210	–79,1	370
Profit attributable to shareholders before extraordinary item	**7 177**	6 735	+6,6	15 632
Extraordinary item (goodwill)	1 533	1 539	–	3 500
Profit attributable to shareholders	5 644	5 196	+8,6	12 132
Weighted number of ordinary shares in issue	13 309 852	13 154 715		13 154 715
Earnings per share	53,9	51,2	+5,3	118,8
Interim dividend (cents)	14,5	14,0	+3,6	14,0
Final dividend (cents)	–	–		21,0
Dividend cover (times)	3,7	3,7		3,4

Financial
The slowing down in economic activity has been accompanied by a general destocking as a consequence of high interest rates. In spite of this, sales have grown by 20% to R94 million and operating profit is 27% higher than the comparative period. However, the higher interest burden has given rise to disappointing earnings. Earnings per share rose marginally to 53,9 cents, up 5% when compared to the same period last year.

Acquisitions
The group acquired the business of Associated Diesel Holdings Limited ("Adco") effective from 1 July 1989, subject to certain conditions being met. These conditions have now been met but account has not yet been taken of the profits arising from this acquisition in the trading results to 31 August 1989.

Prospects
The earnings per share for the financial year are forecast to exceed those of the year ended February 1989.

Declaration of Dividend No. 28
Notice is hereby given that on 3 October 1989, the directors declared an interim dividend of 14,5 cents per share to shareholders registered in the register of the company at the close of business on 27 October 1989. The dividend will be paid on 10 November 1989.

By order of the Board
DB Riley *Chairman*
GL von Loeper *Managing Director*

3 October 1989

Registered Office
9 Old Main Pretoria Road
Halfway House
Midrand
1685

Transfer Secretaries and Certification Office
Central Registrars Limited
154 Market Street
PO Box 4844
Johannesburg 2000

Directors: DB Riley (Chairman), GL von Loeper (Managing Director), WC Akal, AS Barnes, WP Benz, SJ de Vos, RD Gudegast, BC McCarthy, L Miller, R Norwitz, D Saville, GM Walker for the *whole year* ended February 1989. On the basis of these extremely large interest-bearing loans, what hope can a company have of bettering its previous performance?

Within the short period of only two months, MIDAS' share price of 1400 cents at the time of the results had dropped by half.

However, instead of isolating MIDAS in this regard by paying attention specifically to the unsatisfactory situation of its interest-bearing loans and hence unacceptably high interest charges, various share analysts placed the industry of automotive components under the spotlight. As a result, all four of the shares listed on the JSE operating in this sphere suffered rather severe decreases in their share prices.

In summary, I stress once again the importance of my Laws 6 and 7 regarding the financial pedigree of the companies whose shares the investor is contemplating purchasing. Companies which flagrantly violate the requirements of these two laws should be avoided.

11.5 The dangers of holding an overvalued share

There is a second lesson to be learnt from the example of MIDAS analysed above. This concerns the dangers inherent in holding an overvalued share.

Just prior to the release of its August 1989 interim results MIDAS was standing at 1400 cents, which on a dividend of 35 cents offered a dividend yield of only 35/1400 or 2,5%, a figure which was exactly half the sector average. Invariably, purchasers of MIDAS justified their actions by referring continually to the vague topic of 'anticipated' results. However, we must take note of the time staggering between cause and effect in such a situation.

The share price here will always be some two to three steps ahead of the dividend which is to justify that price. For example, the price of 1400 cents for MIDAS will at the sector average dividend yield of 5% require a dividend of 70 cents. This means a doubling of the ruling dividend. Even the most ardent MIDAS adherent would admit that this would take at least two years to be achieved.

However, the dangers inherent in the holding of such a share whose price is based on a two-year-hence anticipated dividend become all too evident *if these anticipations do not materialise*. The moment the implications of MIDAS' interim results in figure 11.2 were realised, and this did not even take 24 hours, heavy selling became the order of the day. Daily price decreases of between 50 and 100 cents became the norm, such was the degree of disenchantment among the company's former supporters in the investment community. This verifies my opinion expressed in 9.11: the disillusioned portfolio manager becomes quite ruthless should his expectations regarding a previous favourite on the Stock Exchange prove groundless. He wishes to rid his clients of this stock under virtually any circumstances, and is quite willing to drop his required selling price dramatically to achieve this goal.

A drop in share price of 50% in only two months, which is what happened in the case of MIDAS, can only result in fingernails bitten to the core among the remaining shareholders. It is of interest that MIDAS' price after the drop, that is 700 cents, was precisely that offering the average dividend yield of the sector housing it. Thus a hopelessly optimistic overvaluation of the share gave way to a more realistic and logical value.

Hence the ultimate moral of this aspect of the MIDAS story: beware the dangers inherent in holding an overvalued share. Delightful anticipation in no way justifies an overvalued situation, particularly when this anticipation is of greatly increased dividends way into the future!

12

The private investor and the blue chip share

Page

12.1 Introduction

This is an important chapter. It concerns the taxation pitfalls that the private investor should be aware of when he elects to purchase shares designated as 'blue chip'. A definition of this latter category follows shortly.

By far the majority of financial journalists and investment advisers continually exhort private investors to purchase what are esoterically termed blue chip shares. Rarely, if indeed ever, have I encountered in my reading on the subject a detailed exposition of the tax dangers to which the private investor is exposed when he purchases this type of share. The reason for this omission is possibly that, as is pointed out in chapters 4 to 7, the standpoint of Inland Revenue *vis-à-vis* the private shareholder has rarely been investigated.

Hopefully this deficiency has been resolved in this text. I now proceed to analyse in considerable detail the pitfalls and taxation obstacles which Inland Revenue has placed in the path of the private shareholder who ardently tries to comply with the published exhortations of financial journalists to purchase almost exclusively blue chip shares.

It must be stressed that my remarks are addressed exclusively to the *private investor*. Financial institutions are not subject to these taxation dangers.

12.2 Leading up to the concept 'blue chip' share

In order to convey the fullest possible appreciation of the concept 'blue chip' share, I commence my discussion with the example of the company MIDAS, which is analysed in some detail in chapter 11.

I ask my readers to put themselves in the shoes of a prospective investor in the year 1988. The financial results shown in fig 11.1 indicate that at that stage MIDAS complied with all but one of my laws. The earnings-per-share of 61,2 cents showed a magnificent 76% improvement over the 34,7 cents of the previous year. In addition, the dividend of 20 cents showed an even more impressive 82,2% increase over the 11 cents previously declared. All in all, then, the prospective investor must obviously have been impressed by MIDAS' performance for the year ending February 1988.

The one law which MIDAS did not obey was my Law 4 relating to the acceptable value of the share. MIDAS has consistently been priced far above the average earnings and dividend yield of the section in which it is housed on the Stock Exchange, but we will bypass this aspect for the moment, since it does not play a part in the point which I wish to make.

For the following year, that ended February 1989, we see an even more impressive performance. Earnings-per-share increased by the unbelievable figure of 94% to 118,8 cents, and the dividend by the equally unbelievable 75% to 35 cents. It was precisely at this stage, as I point out in chapter 11, that the sharp-eyed reader would have spotted the horrific rise of 376% in interest-bearing debt. Of course a discerning investor would have been asking the pertinent question whether the sharply increased dividend of 35 cents over the previous 20 cents should not have been reduced somewhat, for example to the quite acceptable increase of only 25%, and the remaining funds used to reduce the debt pertaining.

Be that as it may, we have the impressive rise in earnings-per-share for MIDAS of 34,7 cents to 61,2 cents to 118,8 cents over a period of a mere three years. The average investor who overlooked the sharp rise in interest-bearing debt would surely have been taken by surprise by the drop in performance reflected in MIDAS' results over the following six month period.

If there is one characteristic which the Stock Exchange investor absolutely abhors, it is a sudden change in the previously favourable direction of a company's financial performance. It is this abhorrence which gave birth to the classification 'blue chip' share.

12.3 Definition of a blue chip share

The definition of a blue chip company is based purely on chronology, that is on historical grounds. To most analysts, *a blue chip company is one with an unblemished record of continual financial improvement over the past ten years.*

The phrase 'unblemished record' means that the earnings-per-share and the dividends declared never once decline during these ten years, and preferably show a continual increase for this period.

Now this is an extremely stringent requirement, the degree of which can be appreciated given the information that as of the time of the writing, only some 3% of the 800 shares quoted on the Johannesburg Stock Exchange fulfil it. That is, at my last count, only 24 companies out of 800 satisfied this condition of a ten-year unblemished record. One of the prime reasons for this is that a large number of the listed companies have not been on the boards for ten years. In order to relieve this requirement somewhat, many writers have begun to relax the time stipulation to not less than five years.

On this relaxed definition it will be found that some 5% of companies qualify, that is, 40 companies out of the listed 800 qualify to be classified as blue chip companies.

The reader must be somewhat puzzled at this stage. If a blue chip company is one which has a consistent record of excellent past performance, why am I against the acquisition of blue chip shares by the private investor? The explanation lies in the subtleties and stringencies of the obstacles which Inland Revenue has placed in the path of the private shareholder wishing to obtain the classification of capital gains for the profits he eventually realises on these shares.

In ending this section I hasten to point out that I am not strictly against the acquisition of blue chip shares by the private investor. I merely require that he be fully conversant with the taxation implications thereof. These are explained in considerable detail in this chapter.

To present the crux of the discussions to follow at the very outset, it is that *the dividend yield of blue chip shares is invariably extremely low compared with that of other shares.* Figures of some 2% are commonly encountered, and it is this aspect which causes Inland Revenue's concern, specifically with regard to the private shareholder. For this reason Inland Revenue requires that the private shareholder complies with what I personally consider to be *an onerous time stipulation*. But more of this in what follows.

In order to avoid generalities, I commence with a quantitative consideration of the financial performance of possibly the most renowned of blue chip shares, ANGLOS.

12.4 The bluest of blue chips: ANGLOS

As an indication of what is to be expected from the financial analysis of a blue chip share, I now consider possibly the bluest of all blue chips. This is the company called Anglo American Corporation of South Africa, abbreviated merely to ANGLOS. The share appears in the 'MINING HOUSES' sector on the boards of the Johannesburg Stock Exchange.

Figure 12.1 shows the financial results for the year ended 31 March 1989, with comparative figures for the previous year. From the table headed 'Segmental analysis of equity accounted earnings', which latter esoteric phrase will be explained later, we read that ANGLOS has its interests in the following divisions:

Division	%
Diamonds	25,7
Mining finance	22,8
Industry and commerce	18,8
Gold and uranium	14,8
Platinum and other mining	7,6
Banking, insurance, property	5,3
Coal	3,0

The reason for the popularity of the ANGLOS share is clearly apparent – the shareholder has an extremely wide spread of investment interests. Instead of purchasing individual shares in each of the above subdivisions, by purchasing ANGLOS the shareholder obtains an all-in-one opportunity. It would be difficult to find another listed company with interests as widely spread as those of ANGLOS.

I give a detailed explanation of the concept 'equity accounted earnings' in chapter 8 of my first book, *Winning on the JSE*. In essence, an *associated company* is one in which the parent investment company holds as a long-term investment 20% or more of the issued shares. The 'equity method of accounting' for investments in associated companies is adopted and the investment company claims a portion of the associated company's retained earnings.

The moment we are informed of the presence of associated companies, we recognise that the correct valuation of the share price of the parent or investment company cannot be obtained by means of a consideration of the sector average earnings or dividend yield, as was the case for the industrial company AUTOQUIP dealt with in chapter 3. As mentioned in 3.8, and as explained in considerable detail in chapter 6 of my book *Winning on the JSE*, the acceptable value of such a share is established via considerations of the *net asset market value* per share. We must bear this finding in mind when analysing the financial results of ANGLOS as depicted in figure 12.1.

The first step in the analysis of these results is the recognition that the after-tax attributable earnings *excluding any consideration of the retained earnings of associated companies* is the figure of R1 254 million. The reason for focusing attention specifically on this item is that *ANGLOS is to pay as dividends one half of this amount*. Thus

Figure 12.1 ANGLOS: Results for the year and final dividend

Anglo American Corporation of South Africa Limited

Registration No 0105309 06

Results for the year and final dividend

(subject to final audit)

Consolidated Income statement

(R million)	Year ended 31.3.89	Year ended 31.3.88
Net income		
– investments	**1 282**	1015
– trading	**427**	274
– other	**89**	121
Net income before taxation	**1 798**	1 410
Taxation	**274**	206
Net income after taxation	**1 524**	1 204
Attributable to outside shareholders	**270**	167
Attributable earnings	**1 254**	1 037
Retained earnings of associated companies	1 391	772
Equity accounted earnings	**2 645**	1 809
Extraordinary items	**24**	449
Earnings after extraordinary items	**2 669**	2 258
Transfer to non-distributable reserve	**1 401**	1 258
	1 268	1 000
Ordinary dividends (note 2)	**622**	516
Retained earnings	**646**	484
Number of ordinary shares in issue – millions	**230**	229
Earnings per ordinary share – cents		
– attributable earnings	**545**	453
– equity accounted earnings	**1 148**	790
Dividends per ordinary share – cents		
– interim	**70,0**	62,5
– final	**200,0**	162,5
Net asset value per ordinary share – cents (note 3)	**12 379**	8 536

Segmental analysis of equity accounted earnings

	1989 R million	1989 %	1988 R million	1988 %
Mining finance	**604**	**22,8**	399	22,0
Gold and uranium (including Amgold)	**391**	**14,8**	392	21,7
Diamonds	**679**	**25,7**	350	19,3
Coal	**80**	**3,0**	51	2,8
Platinum and other mining	**200**	**7,6**	140	7,7
Industry and commerce	**498**	**18,8**	293	16,2
Banking, insurance and property	**139**	**5,3**	116	6,5
Total	**2 591**	**98,0**	1 741	96,2
Other net revenue	**192**	**7,2**	175	9,7
Prospecting	**(138)**	**(5,2)**	(107)	(5,9)

The equity accounted earnings have been analysed on a segmental basis show the relative contribution of the various sectors in which the Corporation is invested. This analysis is based on the principal business activity of each investment and so does not indicate the diversity of the underlying investments, details of which will be given in the annual report.

Comment

Equity accounted earnings increased by 46,2 per cent to R2 645 million (1 148 cents per share) from R1 809 million (790 cents per share). One segmental basis the major impetus for this improvement came from the 94,0 per cent growth in diamond income to R679 million (1988:R350 million) so that this sector contributed 25,7 per cent (1988:19,3 per cent) total earnings. Gold was the only sector not to show satisfactory growth contribution remaining virtually unchanged at R391 million and its share total earnings dropping to 14,8 per cent (1988:21,7 per cent). This reflects the static dividend income from gold mining as a result of the sluggish gold price which increased by 9,1 per cent in the 1988 calendar year to R992 oz ($437), compared with R909 ($447) in 1987, while production costs increased at a much higher rate.

Attributable earnings increased by 20,9 per cent from R1 037 million (45 cents per share) to R1 254 million (545 cents per share). This rate of increase is lower than that for equity accounted earnings because of increased profit retention by associates and because the static gold mine income comprises a proportionately higher 29,8 per cent of attributable earnings compared with only 14,8 per cent of equity accounted earnings.

Net income from investments increased by 26,3 per cent to R1 282 million largely because of higher dividends from diamond interests. Trading income increased from R274 million to R427 million reflecting the improved trading conditions experienced by the coal sector. Other net income was lower at R89 million (1988:R121 million) largely because of increased prospecting costs of R138 million (1988:R107 million) and a smaller surplus on realisation of investments. The higher taxation charge of R274 million (1988:R206 million) was attributable to the subsidiary, Amcoal, while the increase of R103 million to R270 million in the interest of outside shareholders in net income after tax arises mainly from the improved diamond and coal earnings. Retained earnings of associates, which are transferred to non-distributable reserve, were R619 million higher at R139 million, an increase of 80,2 per cent. Over one-third of this increase arises from the much higher equity accounted earnings of the diamond interests while industrial and offshore associates recorded significantly improved earnings enhanced by a weaker rand.

For and on behalf of the board

GWH Relly
J Ogilvie Thompson *Directors*

June 2 1989

Head office:
44 Main Street

London office:

dividends for the year ended 31 March 1989 amount to R622 million. Since the number of issued shares is given as 230 million, the dividends per share emerge as 270 cents.

The specific reason for approaching the analysis in this manner is the recognition that the retained earnings of associated companies of R1 391 million are to be transferred to a *non-distributable reserve* as indicated. This means that the sum involved will not be available for distribution as a dividend.

Now comes the crunch. The associated companies play an important role in the determination of the net asset market value of ANGLOS, since it is the latter's shareholding in each of the former companies which features here. In other words, we have the paradoxical situation that the item which determines the acceptable value of the ANGLOS share plays no part whatsoever in the dividend declaration on the part of ANGLOS. *To make matters even worse, ANGLOS will declare as a dividend only one half of its attributable earnings, excluding the retained earnings of its associated companies.*

This, then, is the explanation of the low dividend yield found in the case of the ANGLOS share. We are informed that the net asset market value per ANGLOS share is the figure of 12 379 cents. On a dividend of 270 cents for the year under analysis, the dividend yield is 270/12 379, that is 2,18%. This is regarded as an extremely low dividend yield. The explanation for its existence is as offered above.

As a basis for comparison we see that the previous year's dividends were 225 cents and the net asset market value per share was 8 536 cents, offering a dividend yield of 225/8 536 or 2,6%. The increase in annual dividends was 20%. However, of far greater importance, particularly to those financial institutions holding ANGLOS, is the fact that the increase in the acceptable value of the share, as reflected in the increase in its net asset market value, was the large figure of 12 379/8 536 or 45%.

To indicate the performance expected of a share of blue chip status, figure 12.2 illustrates the financial results six months later. The interim dividend declared of 85 cents is 21% greater than the previous 70 cents, while the net asset market value per share has climbed to 13 713 cents from the corresponding figure of 9 358 cents one year previously. The annual increase here is the magnificent figure of 13 713/9 358, or 46,5%.

We come again to the determination of that item upon which Inland Revenue focuses its attentions, namely the dividend yield. *Even if the investor were to purchase his ANGLOS share at its acceptable value, namely at its net asset market value per share, of 13 713 cents, the dividend yield would be the figure of 285 cents for the most recent 12 month period divided by the purchase price of 13 713 cents, or 2,07%*. This, it must be realised, is an extremely low return in the form of a dividend yield.

12.5 Inland Revenue's quandry regarding the private investor

Often when a private investor has acquired his blue chip share at the conventionally low dividend yield, Inland Revenue can justifiably turn around and state that *this dividend yield was low purely and simply because the purchase price of the share was excessively high*. It must be remembered that by definition the term 'dividend yield' means the yield at the moment of purchase and is therefore given by the magnitude of the dividends declared over the past 12 month period divided by the purchase price of the share. Thus as the latter increases, so the dividend yield decreases.

It must be noted that more often than not Inland Revenue is quite correct in its standpoint here. *But this does not apply in the case of ANGLOS* if the shareholder has acquired his shares at a price closely related to its net asset market value as calculated in the most recently released financial results. It is precisely for this reason that I chose to analyse a financial company such as ANGLOS to make the point under consideration.

12.6 An equitable mathematical solution for Inland Revenue

The stage we have reached is of sufficient importance to warrant a recapitulation of the fundamentals of the taxation aspects.

First and foremost, the correctly operating investor on the Stock Exchange desires that his purchases of shares should be classified as the acquisition of capital assets.

The fundamental dictum that I have used in this text to describe a

Figure 12.2 ANGLOS: Interim report and dividend for the six months ended September 30, 1989

Anglo American Corporation of South Africa Limited

Registration No 01/05309/06

Interim report and dividend

for the six months ended September 30 1989 (unaudited)

Consolidated Income statement

(R million)	Six months ended 30.9.89	Six months ended 30.9.88	Year ended 31.3.89
Net income			
– investments	**632**	476	1 282
– trading	**279**	191	427
– other	**28**	10	89
Net income before taxation	**939**	677	1 798
Taxation	**210**	132	274
Net income after taxation	**729**	545	1 524
Attributable to outside shareholders	**130**	86	270
Attributable earnings	**599**	459	1 254
Retained earnings of associated companies	**716**	559	1 391
Equity accounted earnings	**1 315**	1 018	2 645
Extraordinary items	**29**	70	24
Earnings after extraordinary items	**1 344**	1 088	2 669
Transfer to non-distributable reserve	**751**	614	1 401
	593	474	1 268
Ordinary dividends	**196**	161	622
Retained earnings	**397**	313	646
Earnings per ordinary share – cents			
– attributable earnings	**260**	200	545
– equity accounted earnings	**570**	443	1 148
Dividends per ordinary share – cents			
– interim	**85**	70	70
– final	**–**	–	200

Consolidated balance sheet

(R million)	At 30.9.89	At 30.9.88	At 31.3.89
Ordinary shareholders' equity			
Capital and premium	**231**	167	197
Non-distributable reserve	**6 668**	4 923	5 955
Retained earnings	**4 413**	3 650	3 993
	11 312	8 740	10 145
Preferred capital	**5**	5	5
Outside shareholders' interests in subsidiary companies	**1 271**	1 135	1 245
Total shareholders' interests	**12 588**	9 880	11 395
Loan capital	**194**	210	200
Loans from associated companies and others	**1 845**	1 949	1 834
Other liabilities	**1 266**	856	1 262
	15 893	12 895	14 691
Represented by:			
Investments	**10 360**	8 078	9 224
Fixed assets	**2 327**	2 211	2 280
Stocks and debtors	**1 179**	858	1 092
Deposits and cash	**2 027**	1 748	2 095
	15 893	12 895	14 691
Number of ordinary shares in issue – millions	**231**	230	230
Net asset value – cents per ordinary share (after providing for dividend)	**13 713**	9 358	12 379

Based on the market value of listed investments at September 30 1989 and the directors' valuation of unlisted investments at March 31 1989

Notes:

1. References to ordinary shares, ordinary shareholders and ordinary dividends include the S ordinary shares which rank pari passu in all material respects with the ordinary shares.
2. Particulars of the Group's interests in listed associated companies and general investments are as follows:

	At 30.9.89 R million	At 30.9.88 R million	At 31.3.89 R million
Associated companies			
Market value	**25 791**	17 400	23 575
Carrying value	**7 231**	5 554	6 394
	18 560	11 846	17 181
General investments			
Market value	**4 197**	2 748	3 666
Book cost	**612**	373	433
	3 585	2 375	3 233
Appreciation	**22 145**	14 221	20 414
Outside shareholders' interest therein	**2 970**	2 127	3 429
	19 175	12 094	16 985

3. Particulars of the Group's capital expenditure, which relates almost entirely to the operating subsidiaries, are as follows:

	At 30.9.89 R million	At 30.9.88 R million	At 31.3.89 R million
Capital expenditure for period (net)	**85**	83	203
Capital expenditure commitments (net)	**378**	422	386

4. There are no material changes in contingent liabilities from those disclosed in the latest annual report.

Comment

Attributable earnings for the six months ended September 30 1989 rose by 31 per cent to R599 million (260 cents per share) from R459 million (200 cents per share) for the corresponding six months of 1988. Equity accounted earnings increased by 29 per cent to R1 315 million (570 cents per share) from R1 018 million (443 cents per share). The interim dividend has been increased by 21 per cent to 85 cents per share from 70 cents per share.

Income from investments at R632 million was 33 per cent higher than the comparative R476 million, most of this increase being attributable to higher dividends from the mining finance, diamond, platinum and base metals sectors. As there was a minimal increase in dividend income from gold and uranium mining interests the contribution by this sector to investment income for the six months fell from 38 per cent to 30 per cent. This drop reflects the impact of inflation on costs relative to the marginal improvement in the rand gold price which rose by only 2,1 per cent to R985 per ounce ($384 per ounce) in the first six months of 1989 compared to R965 per ounce ($453 per ounce) in the corresponding period in 1988. The average for the 10 months to October 31 1989 was R990 per ounce ($377 per ounce), although the price has risen recently to over R1 000 per ounce.

Trading income increased by 46 per cent to R279 million from R191 million mainly due to Anglo American Coal Corporation Limited's (Amcoal's) improved results from increased export prices and tonnages and a weaker rand/US dollar exchange rate. A large part of the increase in taxation and of the increase in outside shareholders' interests in earnings is also attributable to Amcoal's improved results. Other net income rose from R10 million to R28 million as higher interest and fee income more than offset increased prospecting costs. Retained earnings of associated companies, which are transferred to non-distributable reserve, rose by 28 per cent to R716 million. The sectors referred to above, together with the industrial sector, were the major contributors.

Although difficult to predict, equity accounted and attributable earnings for the year ending March 31 1990 are expected to show a lower rate of increase than that recorded for the first six months. The expectation of a deceleration in the rate of growth of earnings takes cognizance of the continuing fall in the profitability of the gold mining industry (although the recent improvement in the US dollar price of gold will, if sustained, have a favourable impact), the slow-down in a number of export markets coupled with the slightly firmer rand, and more difficult economic conditions in South Africa.

For and on behalf of the board

GWH Relly
J Ogilvie Thompson *Directors*

Johannesburg
November 24 1989

Dividend

On Thursday, November 23 1989, the directors of the Corporation declared interim dividend No. 107 on the ordinary and S ordinary shares as follows:

Amount (South African currency)	85 cents per share
Last day to register for dividend (and for changes of address or dividend instructions)	Friday, December 22

capital asset is that of *Botha*, JA in 1975 (quoted in 6.2). The crucial portion of this dictum is the phrase:

> . . . or whether the sale constituted the realisation of a capital asset acquired and held for purposes other than such a profit-making scheme.

Consider, now, the private investor who has purchased a blue chip share such as ANGLOS, for example, whose dividend yield at the purchase price is a mere 2%. How is the investor to answer Inland Revenue's inevitable question when ultimately he decides to sell his blue chip?:

> What explanation is there for the requirement of held for purposes other than such a profit-making scheme?

At a dividend yield as low as 2%, the investor most certainly did not acquire his blue chip share for income purposes. Thus we come ultimately to the honest, accurate and obvious finding that the real reason for its purchase was its unquestioned *ability to rise in price.*

The reader must surely appreciate Inland Revenue's quandry. On the one hand, the cautious approach of the blue chip purchaser in ensuring the continuing increase of his capital invested is in no way blamable. On the other, by achieving the latter using the approach adopted, at first sight the shareholder has not complied with the requirements of the definition of a capital asset as stipulated by *Botha*, JA in the dictum quoted in 6.2.

In order to resolve this quandry I put forward the following mathematical solution. I propose a state of affairs *which ultimately will bestow upon the blue chip purchaser the label 'competent investor', despite the initial low dividend yield.*

The sharp-eyed reader will have picked up the use of the word 'ultimately' in the previous sentence. This indicates that the element of time will be used to convert our low-dividend-yield apparently incompetent investor into an acceptable-dividend-yield competent investor.

In essence, the dividend declarations of a blue chip company will conventionally increase at the annual rate of some 20%. This was shown to apply in the analysis of ANGLOS performed earlier.

It must be remembered that the dividend return depends on the initial purchase price of the share, and not any later prices. On this basis let us take the case of a private investor who purchases his blue chip share at a price of 1 000 cents and a dividend yield of 2%. This means that the most recently declared annual dividend was 20 cents.

Inland Revenue looks kindly only at dividend yields in excess of some 5% to classify the shareholder as a competent investor. In other words, Inland Revenue would be looking at a dividend of 50 cents as opposed to the 20 cents received by the shareholder.

I now propose the following. The blue chip dividend of the initial 20 cents should increase at 20% per year. *Let us now impose on our blue chip shareholder the time condition that he retain his share until the total dividends accumulated by him equal what he would have received if he had received a constant amount of 50 cents per year.*

Note that I (and hence Inland Revenue, if it adopts my solution) am being exceptionally lenient here. I am not requiring any annual increase in the figure of 50 cents – I keep this magnitude constant over time.

At the end of each forthcoming year, then, I will calculate the total amount that the blue chip shareholder has received in dividends and compare this figure with what he is expected to receive on Inland Revenue's requirement of a fixed 50 cents dividend per year. In other words, I will compile a table in which the required running totals of dividends received per year are determined. In this table I will increase the blue chip dividend by 20% each year, and then add this figure to the total amount of dividends already received. I will then compare this running figure with the figure that would have accumulated on the constant 5% dividend yield requirement of Inland Revenue. The table appears as follows:

			Inland Revenue's requirement	
Years after share purchase	*Dividend received*	*Running total*	*Dividend received*	*Running total*
1	20 cents	20	50 cents	50
2	1,2 × 20 = 24	44	50	100
3	1,2 × 24 = 28,8	72,8	50	150
4	1,2 × 29 = 34,8	107,6	50	200
5	1,2 × 35 = 42	149,6	50	250
6	1,2 × 42 = 50,4	200	50	300
7	1,2 × 50 = 60	260	50	350
8	1,2 × 60 = 72	332	50	400
9	1,2 × 72 = 86,4	418,4	50	450
10	1,2 × 86 = 103	521,4	50	500

We halt having calculated for a ten year period after the purchase of the blue chip share. Now, for the first time, *the total of dividends received by the investor exceeds the figure Inland Revenue required of him to classify him as a competent investor.*

12.7 The upshot of the argument

We have now reached the final stage of my argument: until the period of ten years has passed, Inland Revenue will not regard a blue chip shareholder as a competent investor. After this period, however, he has discharged the onus placed on him by the dictum of *Botha*, JA, and should he decide to sell his shares, the resulting profits will be treated by Inland Revenue as accruals of a capital nature and hence will not be taxed.

This is the pitfall I mentioned at the commencement of this chapter. *The purchaser of a blue chip share is locked into his share for a period dependent upon the dividend yield of the share at its moment of purchase.* If the latter was the figure of 2%, this lock-in period would be ten years. If the dividend yield at purchase was higher than this, the manner of determining the lock-in period follows that indicated in the construction of the table shown.

Now to some investors the obligation of this lock-in period presents no difficulty whatsoever, and obviously these persons go ahead with their blue chip purchases.

For the private shareholder previously unaware of this blue chip pitfall, I trust the situation has been explained adequately. I also trust that the financial journalists who have always unconditionally recommended the purchase of blue chip shares will now simultaneously make mention of the time onus to be discharged by the shareholder in order to meet the approval of Inland Revenue.

In view of the technique employed, I call this method of converting the low-dividend-yield shareholder into the acceptable-dividend-yield investor that of 'running dividends'.

12.8 For the mathematically inclined

The mathematically inclined reader is bound to dislike the laborious, step-by-step method indicated in the table in 12.6. The knowledgeable will see that the accumulation of the running dividends takes the form of a geometric series, of first term 20, of multiplier 1,2 and of *n* terms, where *n* denotes the number of years for which dividends are to be accumulated.

The required summation of the running dividends for the period of *n* years is:

Equation 12.1

$$\text{Summation} = 20 \times \frac{1{,}2^{n} - 1}{0{,}2}$$

Thus, for confirmation, after the period of ten years for which the table in 12.6 was compiled, this summation is given by:

$$\text{Summation} = 20 \times \frac{1{,}2^{10} - 1}{0{,}2} = 20 \times \frac{6{,}19 - 1}{0{,}2} = 519$$

This figure of 519 must be compared with that of 521 appearing in our previous table. The small discrepancy is due to the rounding-off process that I used in some of the steps in the table; the more accurate figure is the 519 obtained mathematically using equation (12.1).

Finally, the number of years, *n*, for which our low-dividend-yield shareholder will be locked into his share in order to satisfy the requirements of Inland Revenue is given by the solution to the following equation for *n*:

Equation 12.2

$$20 \times \frac{1{,}2^{n} - 1}{0{,}2} = 50 \times n$$

Now we are able to introduce the two dividend *yields* into this equation instead of using the actual dividend amounts of 20 cents and 50 cents. Finally, then, the required number of locked-in years, *n*, to satisfy Inland Revenue is given by the solution for *n* in the equation:

Equation 12.3

$$\frac{1{,}2^n - 1}{0{,}2n} = \frac{\text{minimum dividend yield of Inland Revenue}}{\text{dividend yield at purchase by shareholder}}$$

I trust that equation (12.3) will enable the shareholder of shares with a low dividend yield to calculate simply and rapidly the time onus he has to discharge to Inland Revenue in the form of the number of years for which he will have to remain locked into these shares. This onus is to enable the profits emerging upon the final realisation of the shares to be regarded by Inland Revenue as accruals of a capital nature, and hence to escape tax.

12.9 An interesting occurrence

The compilation of this text has taken me some five years. During this time I have spent at least two years mulling over the type of procedure which would satisfy Inland Revenue concerning the purchase of blue chip shares with a low dividend yield. I came to the final solution of the 'running dividends' method in 12.6 only in January 1990.

Now the remarkable occurrence. For many years now, 20 at least, there has been vehement argument about possible ways of satisfying Inland Revenue regarding the definition and requirements of 'accruals of a capital nature'. For the first time in these 20 years, in his Budget Speech of 14 March 1990, the Minister of Finance proposed the solution that *all shares held for a minimum of ten years would, upon being sold, be free of taxation on the profits thereon.*

No quantitative reasoning was given for this figure of ten years. The remarkable features of this occurrence are, first, my requirement of precisely the same number of years of lock-in period, established mathematically in the table in 12.6, and second, the virtually contemporaneous nature of the findings.

Perhaps it is merely a case of great minds thinking alike!

13

The ziggle effect – the fundamental mode of operation of all price increases on the Stock Exchange

Page

13.1 Introduction

This text is drawing rapidly to a close. However, two important topics remain to be covered. I call the first the 'ziggle effect'. In more esoteric circles it is referred to as the 'technical reaction', but I prefer the far more picturesque connotations of the word 'ziggle'. The second is the 'eesl effect' and is discussed in chapter 14.

The ziggle effect describes the fundamental mode of operation of all share price increases on any Stock Exchange. All share prices will and indeed must ziggle on their upward paths. I explain exactly what I mean by this in this chapter.

13.2 The ziggle effect

As the result of a good set of financial results, the price of a share rises. Invariably, for various reasons including intangible emotional responses on the part of the shareholder, experimental observation shows that the following sequence of events takes place.

Conventionally, the share price increases without hesitation by some 20% upon the publication of a good set of financial results. Once this new figure has been attained sellers appear on the scene and, quite illogically in my opinion, offer their shares for sale. Thereupon the share price begins to fall, and once again experimental observation shows that *the share price drops by about 30% of its recent rise.*

Let us take, for example, a share standing at 200 cents just before the release of its financial results. The share is subjected to detailed analysis by the cognoscenti, who conclude that these results are indeed favourable, their analysis being based on the contents of chapter 3 of this book, and simultaneously receives favourable comment in the daily financial press. As a result it does not take long for the price to reach some 240 cents – an increase of 20% has occurred.

It is at this stage that sellers appear on the market, conventionally offering only small quantities of the share for sale. These are sufficient to halt the uptrend in existence prior to the appearance of the selling instructions, and consequently the share price begins to decrease for the reasons described in chapter 9. Quite remarkably, this drop will continue for some 30% of the recent rise in price. Thus, for example, in the case being considered of a 40 cent increase in the starting price of 200 cents, the result of the selling order will depress the price by 30% of 40, or 12 cents and the share price will decrease to some 240 – 12, or 228 cents. For some inexplicable reasons which have often surprised me in their consistency, once this drop of 30% of the recent rise has been attained, buyers once again appear on the scene and the share price resumes an upward trend.

I repeat that the consistency with which this pattern of behaviour in the share price occurs, is quite astounding. It is illustrated in graphical form in fig 13.1. The reason why I term this graph the ziggle effect is clearly evident: the share price is seen to ziggle in its upward path.

Due to the operation of the ziggle effect, share prices never merely rise. An investor who appreciates this feature will be saved considerable despondency based on the occurrence of a ziggle. I treat this aspect in detail in the following sections.

13.3 My explanation for the occurrence of the ziggle effect

It cannot be denied that the ziggle effect actually occurs. Experimental observation is sufficient to show this.

Figure 13.1 Graphical illustration of the ziggle effect

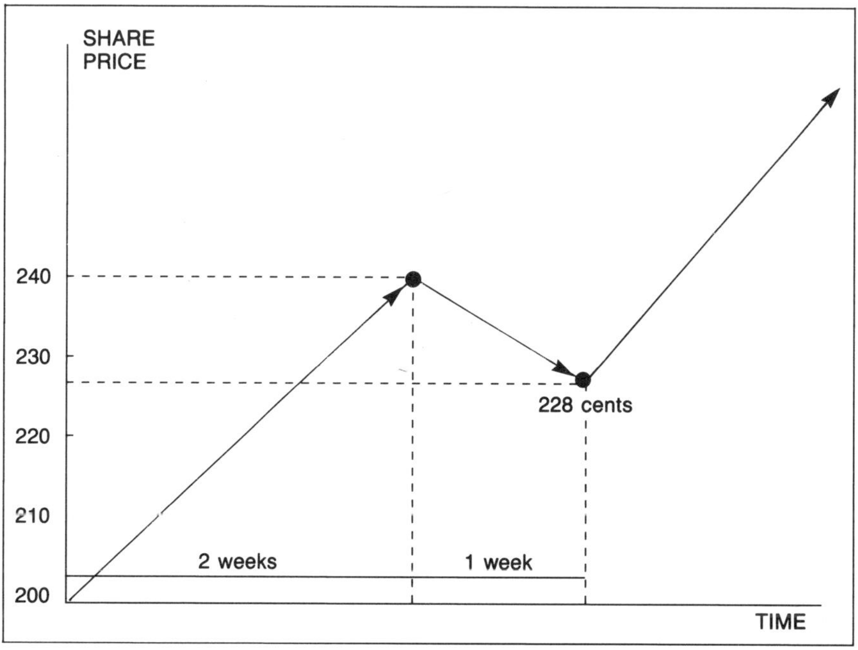

However, what is pure surmise is the postulated explanation for this mode of behaviour on the part of the share price. I now offer my explanation. The reader may have other suggestions which are totally different from mine. I do not object in the slightest; the crux of this discussion is recognition and appreciation of the ziggle phenomenon in share prices.

I am of the firm conviction that by far the majority of private investors on the Stock Exchange are *unable to interpret, and hence appreciate, a good set of financial results*. How these persons became involved with the share under analysis in the first place is an interesting question. Be that as it may, as a result of the recent rise in their share price these 'investors' have achieved conventionally a 20% to 30% annual increase in price, and now become jittery about the prospect of their 'good luck' continuing.

With regard to all Stock Exchange operations, there is a saying to the effect that no one has suffered a loss upon taking a profit! Being ardent protagonists of this attitude, these shareholders begin to sell their shares precisely at the point when all logical analysis of the often highly favourable set of most recently released financial results virtually begs them to retain the shares.

I have often come across the completely inexplicable occurrence that the better the financial results, the more ardently this type of shareholder wishes to dispose of the share. It appears that he just cannot believe his luck, since that is all that it can be termed, in possessing a share which is performing well. He wants to tempt Fate no further, and hence puts in his selling order.

I stated earlier that when this illogical bout of selling ceases, knowledgeable buyers appear on the scene and the share continues its briefly interrupted upward trend. On some occasions, however, the deleterious effect of the ignorant seller is not as simply and rapidly neutralised. It often happens that the occurrence of what can only be termed injudicious selling interrupts for some considerable period a price rise which was gathering momentum and, for good quantitative reasons, seemed set for a further rise of well deserved and considerable proportions.

It is for reasons such as these that I literally beg the ignorant Stock Exchange participant to stand back until his state of knowledge is such that his actions will not affect adversely his fellow participants.

Popular terminology refers to such an ignorant person as 'the little man', and often it is the little man who completely wrecks at the start what was a deserved and promising upward trend in a share price. As I show in the next chapter, it is also this ignorant little man who causes excessive rises in share prices, as occur, for example, during a rampant bull market. Without his support a bull market just could not reach the completely illogical stampeding stage, which latter directly precipitates disastrous crashes in excessively high prices.

To summarise, it is the ignorant Stock Exchange participant who causes undue and unwarranted behaviour in share prices. Ideally this 'little man' should be barred from dealings until he has obtained some form of 'entrance qualification'. Of course this is a most impractical set of circumstances and hence as a more practical solution I can but hope that he will use this and other, similar texts to try to achieve the state of knowledge required of him.

It seems to be the case, then, that in Stock Exchange operations the non-cognoscenti inevitably impede and unduly obstruct the progress of the cognescenti. This, then, is the curse of a supply and demand set of circumstances, which is the very basis of correct Stock Exchange operation, as illogical as this statement may seem to be.

13.4 The importance that the newcomer recognises the ziggle effect

Often I have been telephoned in the following situation. A newcomer to Stock Exchange investment has just purchased his first-ever shares in a company which obeys implicitly my laws set out in chapter 3. As expected, for the following two or so weeks the share price has increased and our fledgling has become sufficiently enthusiastic as to phone his broker at least three times a day to enquire about the latest price of his acquisition.

Believe it or not, his daily mood and his relationship with both his colleagues and his family comes to be determined by the good progress being achieved by his share. A continued rise in its price makes him a most affable employee or employer and a most loving husband and father!

However, the day comes when his telephone call evokes news of a share price decrease since the previous day. The investor acts as if the sky is falling in and become irritable and abrupt, chastising himself for being stupid enough to enter the Stock Exchange. His colleagues are quick to spot the personality change, as is his family. The saviour in this situation is recognition that the inevitable ziggle effect has commenced. Once the newcomer understands and accepts this phenomenon, of which previously he was completely unaware, his attitude to life changes and once again he is able to appreciate the sunshine out there!

I can only state from my experience of being telephoned in such situations, that it is remarkable how share price movements affect the normal daily lives of investors. Maybe psychologists should make a detailed study of the personality of investors in order to alleviate what could become a potentially serious situation.

This, then, is precisely the reasoning for the title of this book. On the basis that fear rests upon ignorance, and that due study and understanding is capable of removing this ignorance, once again I ask the correctly operating Stock Exchange participant to *enjoy* his investment venture.

If his share has been chosen according to my nine laws in chapter 3, and once he has recognised and understood the ziggle effect, all he has to do is relax and enjoy his investment. His share will increase in price and in the process will experience numerous ziggles. He must merely be prepared for the latter occurrence.

13.5 Numerous further ziggles in the share price

The investor must not expect only one ziggle in the upward movement of his share price. He must be prepared for this upward path to adopt the pattern shown in figure 13.2. In other words, for every substantial increase in share price, that is of the order of some 20%, he must expect a ziggle to occur. It is as if the ziggle is a testing ground set by shareholders. This outlook is, of course, the fundamental basis of the Stock Exchange analyst termed the 'chartist'. I leave this weighty and lengthy topic to my following volume, which deals at length with the aims and methods of charting. Hence its title, *Sophistication on the Stock Exchange*. For the moment, however, all that is necessary is for the investor to interpret correctly the share price movement depicted in figure 13.2.

I now introduce the reader to the two basic concepts of the chartist, namely the resistance level and the support level, which arise as follows.

Figure 13.2 indicates the commencement of a share price rise as discussed in 13.2. Having increased suitably, the price drops to point A and thereafter recommences its increase. *A* is termed a 'support level' since at this price the share found sufficient support from enthusiastic buyers to reverse its downward trend and recommence its previous upward path.

The chartist pays special attention to the moment that this now resumed increase in share price exceeds its previously attained maximum. Thus, for example, once point B, representing the previous maximum price,

Figure 13.2 Introducing the concepts 'resistance level' and 'support level'

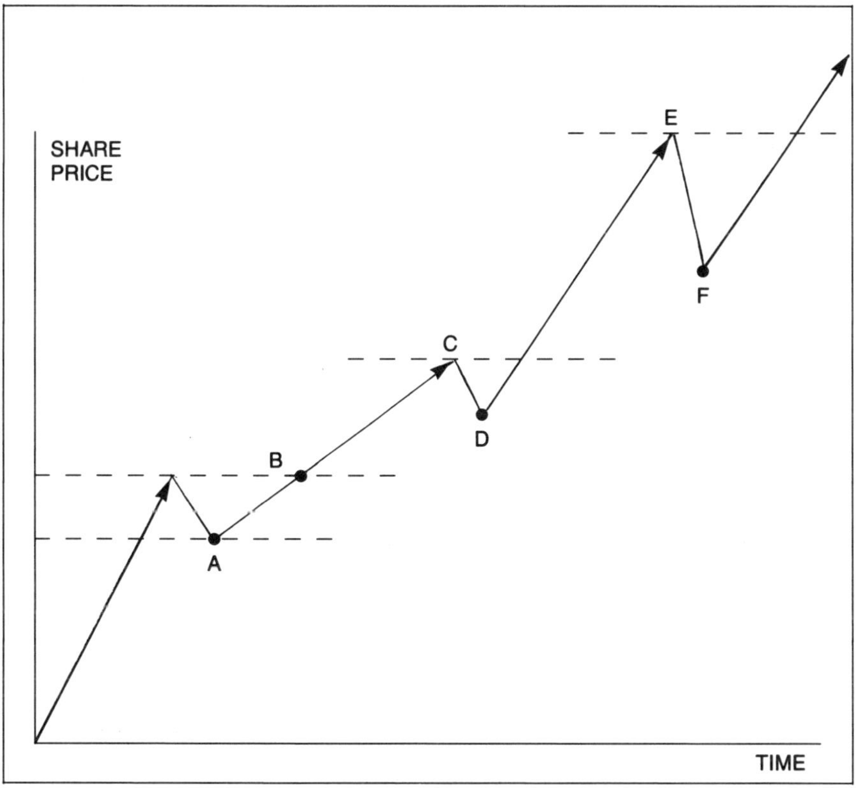

is exceeded, the chartist becomes very enthusiastic about the share's future prospects. *B* is referred to esoterically as a *resistance level*, since the share price has proved able to counter and surpass its previous maximum. Thus the term 'resistance' is very apt.

Fundamentally, the chartist's approach comprises attention to support levels, on the one hand, and resistance levels, on the other. *A fundamental requirement of the chartist is that a support level should never be broken*. In other words, he sees warning signals as soon as the share price drops to a point lower than a previous support level.

The breaking of a previous resistance level is a reason for jubilation on the part of the chartist. The share price is advancing to new heights and hence, according to him, the outlook is very promising.

As I show in my next book, I do not necessarily agree with all the chartist's concepts, although I do admit the importance of some of them.

To summarise this chapter, all that I ask of the correctly operating Stock Exchange investor is that he is aware of the phenomenon I term the ziggle effect and that he recognises its fundamentally psychological, as opposed to quantitative or mathematical, origin.

14

The 'eesl' effect ensures that the ride is never an easy one

14.1 Introduction

Throughout this text I continually urge the reader to enjoy his investment campaign on the Stock Exchange. To make this possible, I offer three suggestions. The first involves the choice of a suitable share, and in this regard I put forward the notion of a company of suitable financial pedigree. The use of my nine laws will assist greatly in recognising such a suitable company.

Thereafter I indicate at great length the procedures which will ensure that the correctly operating Stock Exchange investor befriends and remains friends with, that all important body, Inland Revenue.

My third suggestion is that the investor must recognise that the price of a share will never just rise and continue to rise in a smooth upward path. Chapter 13 introduces and explains the psychological effect which I term the ziggle. Recognition of the existence of the ziggle effect should remove feelings of doubt or discomfort which might otherwise overtake our investor.

However, my readers should note that in all these discussions *I have never once indicated that the ride of the correctly operating investor on the Stock Exchange will be an easy one*. The reasons why constitute the subject matter of this chapter.

14.2 The 'eesl' effect

The reader will have heard of an artist's easel. Here I use a word that is pronounced the same way, but spelt differently. Since 'eesl' is of my own fabrication, let me explain what it means. It is my abbreviation for the phrase '*excessive exuberance sans logic*', and as I will show, its presence virtually ensures that a Stock Exchange journey is never a comfortable one.

In the previous chapter I vent my anger at ignorant investors who depress the price of a share by selling at the wrong moment – just when results warrant their holding the share. I blame the little man, as he is customarily defined in Stock Exchange parlance, for these actions.

Now, however, I vent similar feelings for precisely the opposite behaviour. That is, here I consider and vent my anger at those persons *who are responsible, by their quantitatively unfounded and completely over-enthusiastic buying orders, for the excessive rise in a share price*. Hence my use of the eesl phenomenon as the cause of the price of a share being pushed far beyond the figure that all logic and quantitative analysis would indicate is a reasonable price. Therefore when I refer to a 'price caused by the eesl effect', I mean a share price which has come about purely and simply as a result of excessive exuberance on the part of the buyer, *sans* all logic and the relevant quantitative considerations which normally pertain.

It is the eesl phenomenon which ensures that the investor's ride on the Stock Exchange is never a smooth one. Obviously this point of view warrants detailed discussion and elaboration.

14.3 Stock Exchange price movements are always cyclical

The topic of investor sentiment towards the Stock Exchange as a whole is an extremely involved one. To simplify matters, however, it may be said that basically two prime requirements are necessary for an aura of favourable sentiment to rule. The first is an adequate supply of funds to the relevant financial institutions, and the second is the emergence of consecutive sets of wholly favourable financial reports. That is, company after company must report relatively large increases in earnings-per-share and in consequent dividend declarations.

A third condition on the Johannesburg Stock Exchange, in particular, is that the gold price remain buoyant. The purely psychological reasoning underlying this requirement is too detailed for elaboration at this juncture, and so I request of my reader that he merely accept this notion at present.

With these three requirements fulfilled, the Stock Exchange as a whole will be seen to rise, rather slowly initially, but progressively gathering steam thereafter. On the basis that nothing succeeds like success, the aura of enthusiasm now pervading the Stock Exchange fuels itself rapidly. Instead of a share price rise of my requirement of a 'mere' 40% per year, *rises of some 20% per month occur.*

Now let us review rather slowly and in greater detail how this state of affairs comes about. First, the requirement of adequate funds to the relevant financial institutions means that a home has to be found for these funds. The inflation rate of a typical South African family being of the order of 30%, as indicated in chapter 2, the placement on the Stock Exchange of these large amounts available to institutions follows as a natural and logical solution. The emergence of favourable company financial reports most certainly strengthens the decision of many portfolio managers to take this route of fund placement. As such their decisions can only be praised, *subject, however, to one prime stipulation which is of such importance that it warrants repeating.*

This stipulation is that no matter the extent of the funds available to any one such financial institution, *its portfolio managers do not commit them to causing totally unreasonable increases in share prices.*

14.4 Enter the little man

The financial institutions with their cash flushness are responsible for the first 30% to 50% of the increase in share prices which now become common. Thereafter the little man, bless him in all his ignorance, enters the market at precisely the wrong moment and causes bedlam and havoc.

The Stock Exchange investor of long experience has a very convenient technique of determining when a situation of eesl is about to enter the market. He pays attention to the conversation of typists and clerks and the people he travels with in the lift to his office every morning. If it revolves around how much money is to be made on the Stock Exchange, he can be sure that eesl is imminent.

The emergence of this 'typist and lift syndrome' is so rapid and definite that it has to be experienced to be appreciated. Office conversation centres around nothing but how much each participant 'made' yesterday by the rise in a certain share price and how easily this profit was achieved. A telephone call to a stockbroker is all that is required. Apparently no knowledge or analysis is necessary.

And so the Stock Market stampede is fired and continues to be fired at an ever-increasing pace. Until . . .

14.5 A discussion of the October 1987 JSE debacle

A quantitative indication of the state of affairs at the peak of the debacle which occurred on the Johannesburg Stock Exchange in October 1987 serves to illustrate what I refer to in the previous section.

In the table below I take a number of recognised blue chip shares and show their ruling prices at the peak of this market. I also show the ruling dividends and earnings-per-share to indicate the excessive nature of the share prices.

I have been extremely fair in compiling the above table in that I have taken only those industrial shares which are accepted by the investment community as being shares of standing. Most of them feature in the portfolios of the large financial institutions and by paying attention to them I am most certainly performing a well-reasoned analysis.

Most share analysts become extremely uncomfortable and jittery in the presence of price:earnings ratios in excess of 15. In fact, most

Share	Maximum price attained (cents)	Dividend (cents)	Earnings-per-share (cents)	Dividend yield	P.E ratio
SA BREWS	2 625	50	112	1,9%	23,4
CADSWEP	3 200	75	172	2,34%	18,6
ALTRON	9 000	81	250	0,09%	36
ALTECH	19 000	190	609	1,0%	31
ANGLO AMERICAN INDUSTRIAL	7 400	190	516	2,6%	14,3
ARGUS	13 000	375	902	2,88%	14,4
AFROX	2 375	61	114	2,57%	20,8
AFCOL	1 800	50	100	2,77%	18
PLATE GL	5 150	145	305	2,8%	16,9
BIVEC	1 700	32	98	1,88%	17,3
I&J	2 150	38	122	1,8%	17,6
BLUE CIRC	1 650	39	73	2,36%	22,6
PICKNPAY	5 000	108	220	2,16%	22,7
KERSAF	1 800	52	82	2,9%	22
WALTONS	560	7	22	1,25%	25,5
FOSCHINI	51 000	1 077	2 536	2,1%	20,1
WOOLTRU	1 900	60	118	3,16%	16,1
OK	2 000	73	123	3,65%	16,3
PPC	2 000	60	138	3,0%	14,5
SAFREN	3 500	110	229	3,14%	15,3
SASOL	1 575	47,5	94	3,02%	16,8
SUNBOP	825	27	35	3,27%	23,6

professionals regard the figure of 13 as the absolute maximum at which they are prepared to retain the share under analysis. *This means that a share with a price:earnings ratio of 22 is standing at a price 22/15 or 47% above its absolutely maximum acceptable figure.* On the dividend yield aspect, the lowest figure conventionally accepted with equal comfort is some 3,5%. *This means that a share on a dividend yield of a mere 2% is 3,5/2 or 75% above its maximum acceptable share price.*

Taking this as a basis, look at the comparable figures in the table above. The obvious question, surely, is how on earth the completely excessive share prices shown came about? Since it is only the buyers' price that can move a share price upwards, the answer, expressed extremely succinctly, must be *an overdose of the eesl phenomenon.*

Instead of examining the whole table in minimal detail, I will analyse only one of the shares in the required detail. I choose the share which is possibly blue chip number two in the hierarchy topped by ANGLOS (see chapter 12), namely SOUTH AFRICAN BREWERIES.

14.6 Considering the situation of SA BREWS

As mentioned above, if ANGLOS is blue chip share number one, as I allege in chapter 12, then with complete accuracy SA BREWS may be considered blue chip number two. Despite this rating, the maximum price it attained during October 1987, 2 625 cents, being a price:earnings ratio of 23,4 and a dividend yield of 1,9%, is absolutely unforgivable. It is, as indicated earlier, the epitome of the eesl effect operating at full steam. On the basis of a maximum price:earnings ratio of 15, this means that *the price of 2 625 cents is 23,4/15 or 56% above the acceptable maximum.*

One method of proving my standpoint here is by comparing the maximum price:earnings ratios in other years, both prior to and after the October 1987 debacle. These values are as shown in the table below.

	1985	*1986*	*1987*	*1988*	*1989*	*1990*
Maximum share price (cents)	905	1 700	2 625	2 200	2 750	3 370
Earnings per share (cents)	80	83	112	147	187	202
Maximum price: earnings ratio	11,3	20,5	23,4	15	14,7	16,7

In 1986 knowledgeable investors were already taking note of the commencement of that state of affairs which warrants the closest of attention, namely the type of market termed a 'bull market', with SA BREWS already standing at a price:earnings ratio of the high 20,5.

In passing I have often wondered why this most illogical of situations is termed a bull market. I think I have found the answer, but it is of such a form that I dare not commit it to print! Very politely, I state that it is the eesl effect working overtime.

14.7 The inevitable occurrence of eesl

The highly illogical peak of a bull market cannot endure. It takes some trivial piece of news in South Africa or elsewhere in the world to send it crashing down. In the case of the October 1987 debacle, it was a sudden drop in Wall Street share prices for the most ridiculous of reasons – computer ordered selling.

Two years after this Wall Street 'crash', as it is termed, analysts are still shaking their heads in disbelief at the trigger mechanism of computer based selling orders, which caused fears of another 1931 type depression among Stock Exchange participants. A mere year after the October 1987 crash, prices were rising once again, to cause what the financial press term the shortest bear market in history.

The occurrence of eesl is continuous, but hopefully the periods between its raising its undesirable head will lengthen as the degree of competence of Stock Exchange participants increases.

The phenomenon eesl can be depicted graphically as shown in figure 14.1. The dotted line AY indicates the acceptable growth pattern of 40% per annum. At A, for the combination of reasons discussed in 14.3, an excessive rise in the price of the share commences. This quickly becomes self-fuelling and some 15 to 18 months later point B is attained. The rate of the share price increase due to the eesl phenomenon cannot be sustained, and upon logic returning to the market the very sharp drop BC occurs. In 1987 this was of the order of 40% of the maximum share price achieved. At this stage utter panic and feelings of doom are the order of the day. At the same time, however, it must be noted that an *apparently sharp drop of 40% is merely what is required, on the basis of respectable values of the price:earnings ratio, to bring the share price back to a logical level.*

When point C is reached, for some reason or other a calm sets in among Stock Exchange analysts and suddenly things are not as bad as they seemed. Once again favourable company reports are noticed and assessed in the spirit of logic that they deserve. Lo and behold, the share price resumes its upward trend.

Slowly but inexorably, this initial momentum increases until the previous maximum share price of point B is exceeded. Ultimately point D is attained, with even more favourable financial reports emerging. Then what happens? Yes, dear reader, the eesl debacle strikes once again and the whole cycle is repeated. But this time the crash to point E represents a share price considerably higher than the previously attained C. Once E is reached . . . The reader is quite definitely in a position to ascertain the inevitable for himself.

In figure 14.2 I show the movement of the SA BREWS share price between June 1987 and December 1989. This is the epitome of the

Figure 14.1 The cyclical nature of the eesl phenomenon

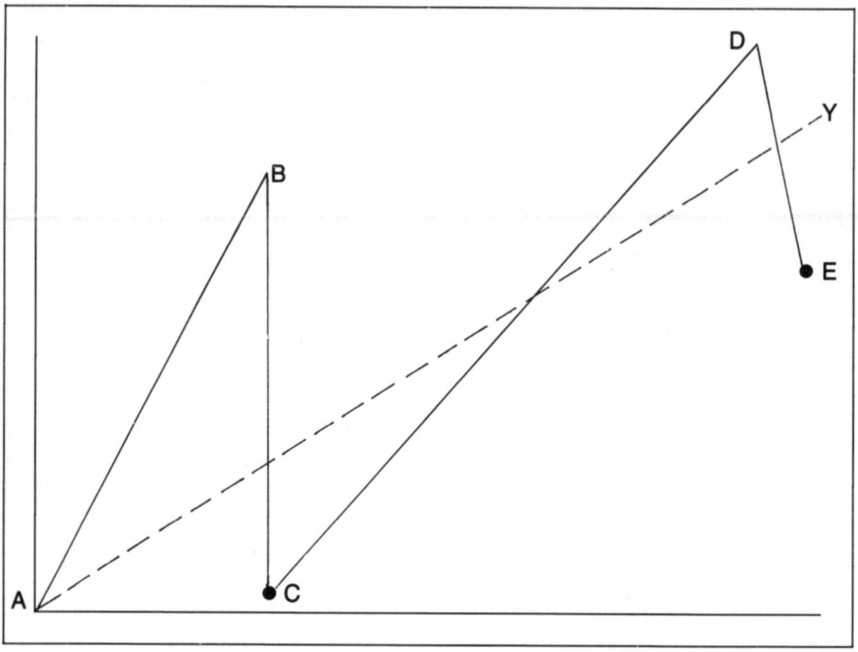

Figure 14.2 Illustration of the persistence of the upward trend in the SA BREWS share price, despite periodic interruptions

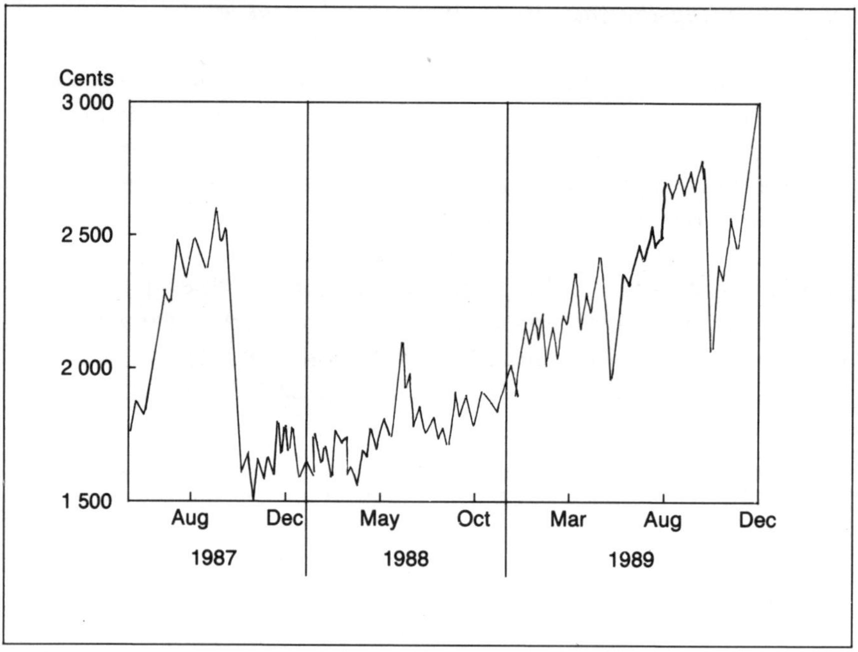

cyclical process I have described. It must be noted that in October 1989, almost exactly two years after the October 1987 crash, yet another sharp drop in the share price occurs. However, having endured this decrease, for example to point E of figure 14.1, the price resumes its upward trend.

In other words the ride on the Stock Exchange will always be a bumpy one, dependent upon the eesl effect. But new highs will always be greater than previous highs, and new lows will always be higher than previous lows. Thus we trust that the upward trend which has endured since the commencement of the Johannesburg Stock Exchange will continue.

14.8 Conclusions

I end this chapter with some rather humorous yet simultaneously very serious remarks made about the bull market by the well-known American share analyst Ian Lamont. He states that as far as shares are concerned, two games are being played – the beauty contest and the greater fool theory.

> The beauty contest game was Keynes' description of investment. You do not choose what you consider to be the most beautiful girl/share, but what you think the judges of the contest – that is other investors – will choose.
>
> The greater fool theory is that you can buy an over-priced share as long as you can be sure that someone even more stupid will buy it off you.
>
> As the bull market develops so confidence will grow, and people will turn to second line stocks because they perceive them to offer better value. Of course, if the bull market runs full cycle, caution will be thrown to the wind and there will be a free-for-all. At that stage the judges' verdict counts for nought, and many of the contestants on the stage will be transvestites!

'Nuff said about the mob or herd psychology when both greed and ignorance fuel the fires.

15

Closing the circle

Page

15.1 Introduction

This text has been written 'live' with regard to the purchase and performance of AUTOQUIP shares. This is to say, on the day that I purchased these shares in March 1989, as detailed in chapter 3, that chapter was written. No benefit of hindsight was obtained.

It is for this reason that I have waited for the appearance of AUTOQUIP's interim results, one year on, before writing this chapter. The interim results are given in figure 15.1, and as far as I am concerned show that the method indicated in chapter 3 and other discussions (see chapter 8) has produced the desired results. It remains for me to analyse, in the normal manner detailed in chapter 10, AUTOQUIP's interim results for the six months ended 31 December 1989.

15.2 Detailed analysis of figure 15.1

The results of the company called MIDAS, shown in chapter 11, really brought a cloud of no confidence over the automotive components industry. It was left to the results of AUTOQUIP, given in figure 15.1, to lift this cloud.

☐ Step 1 Unlike my analysis in chapter 10, I commence here with a consideration of the actual turnover achieved. At R21,667 million it is a very satisfactory 32% greater than the previous R16,413 million. This means that at the very least,

Figure 15.1 Autoquip Group Limited's interim report and declaration of dividend for the six-month period ended 31 December 1989

AUTOQUIP GROUP·LIMITED

(Incorporated in the Republic of South Africa)
(Registration No 87/02838/06)

Interim report and declaration of dividend for the six month period ended 31 December 1989

Turnover	**+32%**
Operating income	**+35%**

Financial results

The consolidated unaudited results are as follows:

Consolidated income statement

Year ended June 1989 R000		Half-year ended December 1989 R000	December 1988 R000	% change
35 546	Turnover	**21 667**	16 413	+32
5 205	Operating income	**2 974**	2 200	+35
583	Finance charges	**466**	161	
4 622	Net income before taxation	**2 508**	2 039	+23
2 161	Taxation	**1 118**	843	
2 461	Net income after taxation	**1 390**	1 196	+16
53	Share of associated company's earnings	**30**	20	
2 514		**1 420**	1 216	+17
3	Outside shareholders' interest	**15**	–	
2 511	Net income attributable to shareholders	**1 405**	1 216	+16
1 040	Dividends	**480**	400	
1 471	Retained income	**925**	816	
16 000	Number of shares in issue (000)	**16 000**	16 000	
15,7	Earnings per share (cents)	**8,8**	7,6	+16
6,5	Dividend per share (cents)	**3,0**	2,5	+20

Consolidated balance sheet

June 1989 R000		December 1989 R000	December 1988 R000
	Capital employed		
4 857	Stated capital	**4 857**	4 857
2 500	Distributable reserve	**3 425**	1 845
7 357	Shareholders' funds	**8 282**	6 702
3	Outside shareholders' interest	**18**	–
350	Medium-term liabilities	**265**	211
7 710		**8 565**	6 913
	Employment of capital		
1 174	Fixed assets and investments	**1 410**	1 146
6 536	Net current assets	**7 155**	5 767
19 648	Current assets	**22 344**	16 496
13 112	Current liabilities	**15 189**	10 729
7 710		**8 565**	6 913
46,0	Net tangible asset value per share (cents)	**51,8**	41,9

COMMENTS:

Profile

The Autoquip division is a wholesaler and retailer of exclusive automotive accessories and performance tyres. The Partquip division is a specialist wholesaler of selective automotive parts whilst the Techniquip division is a distributor of industrial bearings and allied products.

Results

The continued philosophy of niche marketing has ensured that the group has shown real growth in the six months to December 1989. Operating income improved primarily as a result of continued control of costs and purchasing efficiencies.

New developments

A new branch was opened in Port Elizabeth to take advantage of the growth prospects in the Eastern Cape and will facilitate warehousing and distribution for all the divisions of the group.

The Durban warehouse is to be relocated to larger premises in order to cater for future growth.

The Autoquip division in Cape Town is to be relocated from Maitland to the Cape Town city centre in order to be better positioned to take advantage of the disposable income in the area.

Prospects

All divisions will be operating out of our existing warehouse facilities before the end of April 1990 and the board is confident that despite difficult trading conditions our niche marketing philosophy will ensure that earnings in the period to year-end will at least keep pace with those achieved to date.

Dividends

An interim dividend of 3 cents has been declared.
The dividend will be paid on 23 April 1990 to shareholders registered on 12 April 1990.

JI Fleisch
Secretary
29 March 1990

Registered office
6th Floor
Saambou National Bldg
130 Commissioner Street
Johannesburg
2001

Transfer secretaries
Fraser Street Registrars (Pty) Ltd
Ground Floor
65 President Street
Johannesburg
2001

Directors: GJ Santana (*Chairman*), BD Coquelle (*Managing director*), CS Seabrooke, GR Coombes the sales target set by the company has been achieved. Any doubts on this score generated by the disappointing MIDAS results have now been set aside. In other words, the automotive component industry is still alive and well.

- ☐ Step 2 It is one matter to sell adequately; it is quite another for the income accruing from these sales to advance at the same pace. AUTOQUIP has excelled in this aspect in that its operating income, R2,974 million, is the magnificent figure of 35% greater than the previous comparable figure of R2,2 million. In other words, on a 32% increase in turnover, a 35% increase in operating income has been achieved. My congratulations to the management and staff involved!

- ☐ Step 3 Now for the first negative implication. The finance charges to be deducted from this operating income have grown from the previous R0,161 million to the relatively large R0,466 million. In fact, this latter figure is 80% of the R0,583 million interest charges for the entire 12 month period ending June 1989. This aspect warrants some worry.

- ☐ Step 4 The result of step 3 now becomes apparent. The net income before taxation, R2,508 million, is only 23% greater than the previous R2,039 million.

- ☐ Step 5 The tax deducted is at a higher rate, being 1,118/2,508, or a taxation rate of 44,6% compared with the previous 41,3%. The net effect is that the net income attributable to shareholders is only 16% greater than the previous comparable figure. Hence earnings-per-share show a 16% increase compared with the 35% increase in operating income and the 23% increase in pre-tax income. To some this may be something of a disappointment, but as far as I am concerned it represents a perfectly satisfactory figure once its cause is taken into account. Remedial measures are relatively simple to apply.

- ☐ Step 6 The dividend declared shows a welcome 20% increase at 3 cents compared with the previous 2,5 cents. This increase is sure to pacify those investors who are possibly somewhat disappointed with the mere 16% increase in earnings per-share.

☐ Step 7 We come, now, to a consideration of the financial structure of AUTOQUIP. The ratio of medium-term liabilities to shareholders' funds is a mere 0,265/8,282, or only 3,2%. Analysis of other companies reporting for the same financial period shows that figures in excess of 30% are common. This low 3,2% figure is surely indicative of promising performance in the future.

☐ Step 8 With regard to that all-important indicator of company performance, namely the pre-tax return on capital employed, we see that the annualised figure is 2×2,508/8,565, or a magnificent 58,6%. Previously it was 59%. Under the trying conditions implied by the MIDAS results discussed in chapter 11, this represents a great achievement. Figures of some 10% are common in other companies.

☐ Step 9 Regarding future prospects, we read the following statement:

> The board is confident that despite difficult trading conditions our niche marketing philosophy will ensure that earnings in the period to year-end will at least keep pace with those achieved to date.

I am more than satisfied with these prospects.

On the basis of this analysis of AUTOQUIP's December 1989 interim results, the reader may wish me to end this text by merely stating that AUTOQUIP has produced the performance expected and required to satisfy my stipulation of a company of suitable financial pedigree. For these readers I do just that, since the aim of this text has been achieved by the analysis of figure 15.1 and the comparable earlier analyses of figures 3.1 and 10.1. This will close the circle effectively and succinctly, as the title of this chapter indicates.

However, for the enthusiastic reader, while closing the circle of this book I would like to open the circle of my next volume, *Sophistication on the Stock Exchange*.

15.3 The first step in further sophistication: six-monthly graphs

The performance of AUTOQUIP for the period indicated *is actually far better* than indicated by the analyses undertaken in this text. This can be determined by calculating all the relevant quantities at intervals of six months, and then the plotting resultant graphs. The conditions under which this procedure is permitted are discussed in the next volume, and I merely state here that they are fulfilled in the case of AUTOQUIP.

I concentrate, now, on the quantities of the turnover and earnings-per-share for the six-monthly periods indicated in the table below. It should be noted that some of these figures are not given directly in the financial reports in figures 3.1, 10.1 and 15.1, but the reports contain adequate information to permit of their calculation.

	Financial year 1988		*Financial year 1989*		
	Dec 1987	*June 1988*	*Dec 1988*	*June 1989*	*Dec 1989*
Turnover (R million)	10,11	12,053	16,413	19,133	21,667
Earnings-per-share (cents)	4,2	6,3	7,6	8,1	8,8

These figures are actually meaningless as they appear in this table. To interpret and appreciate their significance, it is necessary to plot the graph in figure 15.2. This graph, for the reasons to be discussed, shows incontrovertibly the really magnificent performance achieved by AUTOQUIP during the period indicated.

I discuss the turnover graph first. Correct appreciation of this graph requires knowledge of the really pessimistic surveys of the automobile component industry compiled by share analysts early in 1990. The motivation for these Jeremiah viewpoints was the dismal performance achieved by the company MIDAS as indicated in chapter 11. However, instead of restricting their remarks specifically to this company and accentuating the financial imbalances I indicated in 11.3, analysts incorrectly attributed the poor performance to consumer resistance and similar items.

In this light, then, the turnover graph of AUTOQUIP dispels, for this company if for no other, all fears based on the grounds of consumer saturation. Thus, the rise in turnover from December 1988 to December

Figure 15.2 The performance of AUTOQUIP via its turnover and earnings-per-share in six-monthly intervals

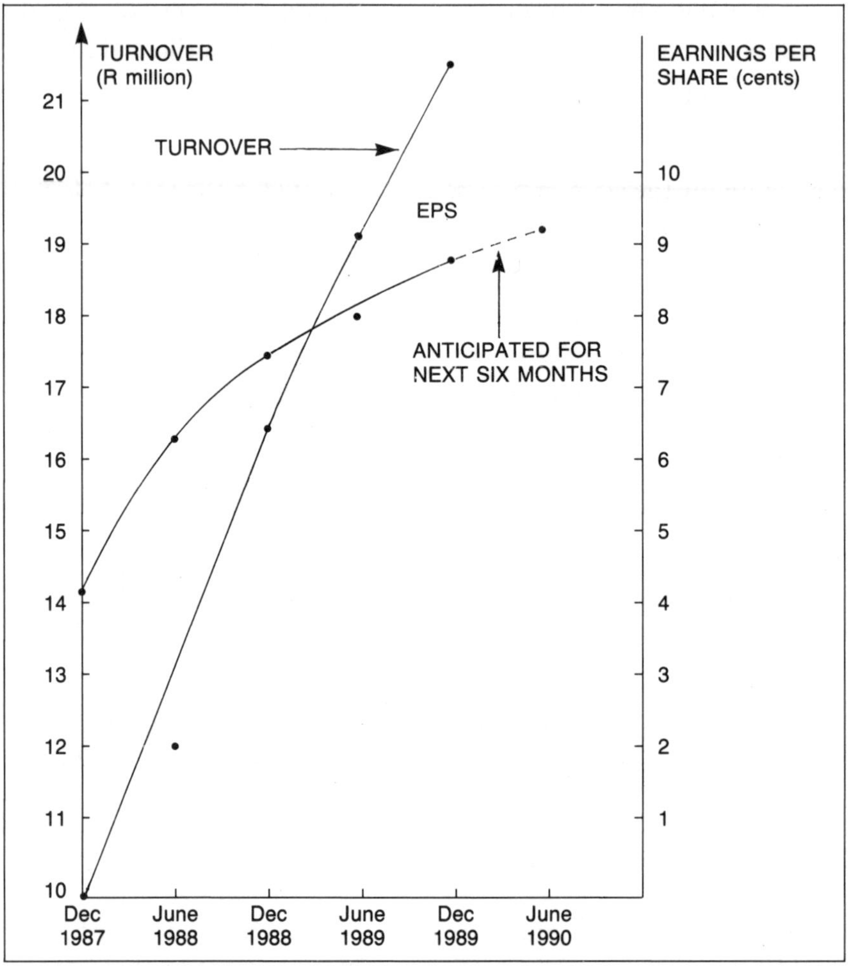

1989 shows only minimal saturation. In fact this saturation is so small that a straight line could equally well have been drawn through these three points on the graph. This bodes well for future performance.

The earnings-per-share graph shows a saturation effect, due primarily as discussed to an increase in the rate of taxation and to increased finance charges. Despite this saturation, the graph is still completely satisfactory.

We come, now, to the possibility of extrapolating the earnings-per-share graph for the following six months. The reasons why this can and cannot be done, are many. Presuming that the former outweigh the latter, and thus that the extrapolation can be performed, it would appear that earnings-per-share of 9,3 cents can be expected for the six months ended June 1990. Let me commit myself to print here, even if I am to be damned in the process!

15.4 In conclusion

I can find no better manner in which to end this text than to state that I trust that I have discharged the onus I placed on myself in the title of the very first chapter. This was: **'Correct Stock Exchange investment is highly erudite'**.

References to judgments of the South African Appellate Division

1 *John Bell & Co (Pty) Ltd v Secretary of Inland Revenue* 1976 (4) SA 415 (A).
2 *Elandsheuwel Farming (Edms) Bpk v Secretary of Inland Revenue* 1978 (1) SA 101 (A).
3 *Commissioner of Inland Revenue v Stott* 1928 AD 252.
4 *Natal Estates Ltd v Secretary of Inland Revenue* 1975 (4) SA 177 (A).
5 *Secretary of Inland Revenue v Trust Bank of Africa Ltd* 1975 (3) SA 652 (A).